I0893118

Contents

My Way

MOANA

HOPE

My Way

MELBOURNE
UNIVERSITY
PRESS

MELBOURNE UNIVERSITY PRESS
An imprint of Melbourne University Publishing Limited
Level 1, 715 Swanston Street, Carlton, Victoria 3053, Australia
mup-info@unimelb.edu.au
www.mup.com.au

First published 2017
Reprinted 2017
Text © Moana Hope, 2017
Design and typography © Melbourne University Publishing Limited, 2017
Images © Moana Hope and individual contributors

This book is copyright. Apart from any use permitted under the *Copyright Act 1968* and subsequent amendments, no part may be reproduced, stored in a retrieval system or transmitted by any means or process whatsoever without the prior written permission of the publishers.

Every attempt has been made to locate the copyright holders for material quoted in this book. Any person or organisation that may have been overlooked or misattributed may contact the publisher.

Excerpts from Eliza Sewell's *Herald Sun* articles on pages 116–17 and 157–8 are reprinted courtesy of the author.

The article on pages 80–81 appears courtesy of Samantha Lane, sports journalist with *The Age* and Channel 7.

Transcripts on pages 95, 97, 98 and 100 courtesy of *Australian Story* on ABC.

The AFL press release on pages 153–4 is reprinted courtesy of AFL Media.

Text design and typesetting by Typeskill
Cover design by Philip Campbell Design
Printed in Australia by McPherson's Printing Group

National Library of Australia Cataloguing-in-Publication entry
Hope, Moana, author.
My way/Moana Hope.

9780522871524 (paperback)
9780522871531 (ebook)

Hope, Moana—Biography.
Women football players—Australia—Biography.

MIX
Paper from responsible sources
FSC® C001695

Kicking off

YOU KNOW THAT feeling you get, when it seems like you're living a dream? That's how I felt in the week leading up to the first game of the AFL Women's competition in early 2017. It seemed completely surreal that it was happening. For so many years women who wanted to play footy had been pushed to the edge of the sporting community. We had been forced to play on any spare cow paddock we could find. We had been seen as freaks. But here we were, on the verge of an official AFL women's competition, with teams being fielded by AFL clubs and the players getting paid to play, rather than us forking out our own money to play, as had always been the case in the past.

On many occasions during that week I found myself pondering if I was really, really going to play for the mighty Collingwood Football Club against its arch-rival, Carlton, at a famous AFL venue, on a Friday night, in a game being televised around the nation by Channel Seven and Fox Footy. To be honest, on a number of occasions I was momentarily gripped by a fear that it was all unreal. That I was going to wake up and find myself back at some suburban ground digging for change to play. But then I would be snapped back into reality by a Collingwood media manager asking me to attend a press conference or a photographer asking me to pose for a photo. And I would smile at the thought that it was really, really happening. I was about to play for the biggest club in Australia, in an AFL competition before a crowd that was being tipped to reach 20,000. It was, to put it mildly, bloody amazing.

The whole week leading up to it was a blur of activity. For a start, I still had to run the traffic management company that is my key source of income. Doing that involves a 3 am start most days to get my crews out on the road in time for the commuter rush. So each day, except on the day of the game, I spent the hours between 3 and 7am working hard before I had time to even think about anything else. As I am also the full-time carer for my disabled sister Vinny, once my traffic management work was done I would spend an hour or so getting her ready to be dropped off to the centre where she is cared for during the day. Then, after all that was out of the way, I had some time for my footy commitments, of which there were many.

On the Monday I did a shoot for Channel Nine's new women's footy show, then I headed off to a shoot for Special K breakfast cereal, as I am now one of their ambassadors. By the time I arrived for training at Collingwood's amazing Holden Centre, I was ready for a nap. But nothing makes me happier than running around with a footy in my hands, so training recharged my batteries. The energy at training that night was like nothing I had experienced before. None of us were taking for granted that we were preparing to be part of history. I think that week all of us in Collingwood's squad had to pinch ourselves at times.

Across the Tuesday and Wednesday I did a photo shoot for a magazine, took part in a segment being filmed for a morning television program, then did a presentation to the staff at CGU Insurance, which is one of Collingwood's major sponsors. Given I was very shy as a kid and really struggled to cope with the way people judged me because of the way I looked during my late teens and early twenties, I found it extraordinary that so many people now wanted to see and hear from me. It made me feel proud of myself and the journey I have taken, and it added to my sense that everything was completely surreal.

I also called in to see our cheer squad making the banner on the Wednesday. The passionate folk who make up the Collingwood cheer squad are my kind of people. A number of them are battlers from the northern suburbs, where I grew up and still live. Like me, they love their families and their footy in equal measure.

On the Thursday morning I did my weekly segment on Gold FM, then fronted a press conference to promote the game with one of Carlton's marquee players, Darcy Vescio. As I was driving back to the club, I was waiting at a red light when the driver in the car next to me started tooting his horn. I thought I must have cut him off or something, so I opened my window to have a chat. He just smiled and said, 'Good luck for your game tomorrow!'

Stuff like that had been happening to me all week. People kept stopping me in the street to wish me luck. It was so beautiful. Three or four years before, I would never have believed that a female footy player would be so recognised and admired that she would be stopped in the street.

At our final training session on the Thursday night, the atmosphere out on the track was electric. The ball hardly touched the ground. Then our team list was released to the public. I immediately logged on to the AFL website to see my name at full-forward. It was a standout moment in an incredible week.

On game day, a Friday, I managed to conjure a rare sleep-in because someone else took over my job so I could rise at 7 instead of 3 am. Once I was up, I just wanted the game to start as soon as possible. Getting Vinny ready for her day helped me relax. She loves to laugh, so we are always mucking around, and it was no different this time. I dropped her off, and then went to my regular cafe to have my favourite breakfast: smashed avocado. I grabbed a copy of the *Herald Sun*. It was mind blowing to see women's footy on the front and back pages. I had even written a column, with some help from one of the reporters, and it was prominently displayed only a couple of pages in from the back. Women's footy had made it to the big time, and I was on board for the ride.

On my way to the Collingwood homeground, I called in to the cemetery where my dad is buried. As I stood by his grave, I imagined how proud he would have been had he been around to see me play for Collingwood. Dad was the one who taught me how to kick and mark and handpass, and who encouraged me to play. I had a little chat with him in my head. I felt like he was going to be right by my side during the game, cheering my every move.

After our arrival at the ground, my teammates and I were taken by bus to Carlton's homeground, Ikon Park. The game was actually meant to be played at our training ground next to the Holden Centre, but the interest in it was so high that it had to be moved to a venue with a much greater capacity.

When we stepped off the bus, the atmosphere was already building. It was a beautiful summer's evening and I could see people dressed in footy jumpers having picnics around the stadium. We walked into our change rooms. Our gear was laid out around the rooms. I picked up my jumper with the number '23' on the back and gazed at it for a minute or so. I picked up a copy of the AFL *Record*, which had been specially produced for the women's competition. There I was on the cover, next to a number of the other marquee players. It was another completely surreal moment. Here I was, about to play for Collingwood.

It wasn't all serious stuff in the lead-up to the game, though. A few of us went out onto the ground before we put our playing gear on and took a selfie, which ended up on the front page of *The Age* the next day. I have never been one to get worked up and serious before a match, so doing these kinds of things helped me get in the right mindset. When we took that selfie, the gates had not yet opened to the public. But by the time we ran out for our warm-up, the stadium was more than half full. The crowd had been greatly boosted by the presence of my family. Around twenty of them had found excellent seats on the wing, where they were accompanied by a crew from ABC's *7.30* program, which was putting together a series of stories about me.

We headed back into the rooms where our coach, Wayne Siekman, reminded us to soak up the occasion and to stick to the game plan that we had spent so many weeks refining. Then it was time to head out for the start of a new era in Australian Rules. There was a minor hiccup when a pole snapped on our banner, which said, 'See the future in black and white. Side by side. History'. I felt really sorry for the members of the cheer squad, but they eventually hauled the banner into shape for us to run through it. As I crashed through and was able to gaze around the ground, I was staggered by the size of the crowd. There was barely a spare seat in the place. I found out later that the AFL had to close the gates during the first quarter because there was no more room for spectators inside the stadium. That meant the crowd had topped 24,500.

The people in the stands cheered our every move as we went through our warm-up. Then we gathered on the northern wing for the national anthem. When it was finished, the crowd went bananas. It felt like the start of a men's AFL Grand Final. We took our positions, the siren sounded and the crowd roared again. Women's football had arrived and my dream of playing footy at the highest level was really coming true. Those bad times in my life, when I had thought about walking away from the game I love and that means so much to me, seemed like an eternity ago.

Part 1

Flashpoint

MIDWAY THROUGH THE 2009 football season, I received a call from the Victorian Women's Football League's (VWFL) media manager, Leesa Catto. She wanted me to take part in a photo shoot for the *Herald Sun*, to accompany an article on the growth of the women's game.

'I'd love to do the shoot,' I told Leesa. She then paused, and said, 'Oh, yeah, but just one thing ... '

'What's that?' I asked.

'We need you to wear a long-sleeved jumper to cover up your tattoos.'

At first the request seemed to go straight in one ear and out the other. I really wanted to take part because, to be honest, I was just buzzed about the prospect of being in the paper. That's all I was thinking about right then. I had been the VWFL's leading goal kicker for the previous three seasons and I felt like this was some recognition of all my efforts. However, the more I thought about what was being asked of me, the more I started thinking the request to cover up my tattoos was outright wrong. She was telling me that I was not allowed to be *me* in the photo. As I thought about this I became angrier and angrier, until I worked myself up into a fury.

At the time I was living at home with my mum, Rosemary, and many of my thirteen siblings. Mum overheard my phone conversation and came in to see me, thinking I would be happy and excited about the photo shoot. But instead she found me sitting on the couch in our lounge room, crying. I told her about being asked to cover up my tatts.

'What's wrong with my tatts? What's wrong with me?' I asked her.

'Nothing,' she replied. Mum was calm when she was comforting me, but she was angry, too—so much so that the next day she wrote a letter to the league about it, but I don't think she ever received a reply. She and I were both adamant that what was being asked of me was a disgrace.

I sat on the couch for what felt like hours. I was in a state of shock. In my mind, I argued with the woman on the phone: 'I'm one of your league's best players, the kind of player that has made people sit up and take notice of the competition, but now you're telling me to change who I am. I just don't understand what I have done wrong to deserve such treatment. I've done nothing but play good football, to the best of my ability. And suddenly you don't like tattoos and short hair? Are you serious?'

Then it hit me. I knew exactly what the request was all about. It was because I looked like a boy. And if you look like a boy you're considered 'butch', and those who run the show were starting to want to manage the 'look' of the game. This was the crux of their concern: how I looked. The VWFL had suddenly decided it wanted to control its image, because everyone thought women's football was full of short-haired, tattooed butch lesbians. The people who ran the league had, out of nowhere, decided they only wanted pretty girls—the ones with clean skin and long hair—to be the face of their competition.

I think what they were trying to do was to promote women's footy to mothers who thought that playing such a rough game was something that girls should avoid. They wanted to reassure these mothers that their lovely girls weren't going to be roughed up by a bunch of tattooed lesbians. The people running the game believed that I could masquerade as one of those pretty girls ... as long as I covered up my many tattoos.

Why should I cover up my tattoos? I thought. Why should I be ashamed of the way I express myself? I sent Leesa a text saying that I thought the idea discriminated against me and that I was pulling out of the photo shoot.

Although I was an emotional wreck for the next couple of days, I eventually pulled myself together, played out the 2009 season and was part of the fourth straight premiership team with my team, the Darebin Falcons. But I now had seriously mixed feelings about football and the people who ran the women's game.

I almost walked away from footy at the end of that year, but my love of the game ran too deep to make such a massive call. So I returned to Darebin and did most of the training in the lead-up to the 2010 season. I then played one game, but after that I found myself in a state of near depression.

Football was the love of my life. Football was my outlet, my place to get away from my crazy home life. Yet I felt like the people running the game were judging me all the time. I felt like they had decided that being a good player was no longer enough. I now had to look the part as well.

Whenever I have moments to just sit and think—when I am not at work, training, playing or trying to keep my siblings and their kids on track—I can go off into a dreamlike state and talk to my dad, Gary. I have always felt that he is still by my side. Dad and I had been so close—like best mates—and he was the one who had encouraged me to play footy and cricket. He had always loved me for who I am. He never judged me if I wanted to play sport with boys. And he never said anything negative to me if I wanted to have short hair or run around with my shirt off when I was a kid, like the boys did. He was my Number One supporter, and he always told me I was better at footy and cricket than most of the boys I faced off against on the field.

At this low time in my life, I was thinking about my dad even more than I usually did. Almost every day I went to the cemetery and sat beside his grave and thought about how being myself was no longer good enough for the league, and cried. I didn't know what to do. Playing footy was my connection to him. When I was out on the field, it felt like he was out there with me. But now a barrier stood in my way. Just the thought of leaving the game weighed on me like a ton of bricks.

Looking back now, I realise Leesa had not meant any personal harm, and I now know she had a totally different perspective, which I talk about later. She was sick of people saying that women's footy was full of butch, tattooed lesbians, when it was a game that attracted women from all sorts of backgrounds and allowed them to play a sport they loved and excelled at. I can now see that, because of all the tired stereotypes about female football players, she was worried I would be portrayed as a cliché, despite my being just a girl who loved playing footy.

Her request that I cover my tattoos had sent me into a spiral. It had made me believe that my favourite sport no longer liked or valued me. That, combined with the fact I was living a crazy life, including being a foster mother to two of my nephews and trying to run my own traffic management business, meant my enthusiasm for football evaporated. I felt deeply hurt. It was like that wounded feeling you have as a teenager when you break up with your first love.

As I pondered my future, I rang my great friend Nicole Graves, who was like a big sister to me. Nicole had been the Darebin Falcons' president in the mid 2000s but was now working in women's football in Western Australia. I told her what I had been going through over the past twelve months, starting with me being told to cover my tattoos, and how it had affected my feelings about the sport I loved. Nicole is a straight shooter, the kind of person who can get the game's hierarchy offside at times by calling things as she sees them. She agreed that I had been treated very poorly. She didn't tell me whether to quit footy or not, she just said, 'You do what you want to do.'

The sad result was that, at a time when I was at the peak of my athletic powers, I no longer felt that footy was a priority in my life. I was so scarred by the way I had been judged that I feared I might never take footy seriously again.

1
Life in the tough lane

I NEVER HAD ANY trouble being me when I was a kid. Sure, I was a bit different from the average little girl. I didn't want to play with dolls or paint my nails. I just wanted to kick the footy or play cricket. I wanted to wear my hair short and run around with my top off. And no one in my family ever wanted to change me. My mum and dad, and my thirteen brothers and sisters, loved me for who I was.

Sure, we had our moments of grief and anger. And we were prone to giving each other politically incorrect nicknames—my brothers called me 'Turkey', because they thought my darkish skin made me look like a Turkish person—but the amount of love I received from them is the thing I remember most about my childhood.

There's no doubt growing up in such a large family was pretty crazy. At one stage, I think there would have been fifteen or sixteen of us living in our two-bedroom housing commission home in the northern Melbourne suburb of Glenroy—my mum still lives there and I haven't moved far, as I am still in the same suburb. But our house was overflowing with love.

Both my parents worked: Dad at a pizza shop owned by my uncle (he and Dad were as close as brothers can be) and Mum at a nursing home. She must have left home quite early each morning to finish around 3 or 4 pm, about the time we arrived home from school. Once Mum was home, Dad headed off to the pizza shop and worked until 1 am or so, making and delivering pizzas.

Even though Mum and Dad both worked, we were such a large family that we only ever had just enough money to get by. We made do with what we had. For Christmas each year, Mum would get a few bags of clothes from an op shop and that would be it. When it came to food, we never ate out. The weekly trip to the supermarket was all we had to get us through.

Going shopping with Mum was a great adventure. There would be at least two trollies piled high with stuff and it would all cost hundreds of dollars. I remember Mum spending $600 on one shopping trip and thinking, 'That's the hugest amount of money I've ever heard of!' But divide that by fifteen, and it's not much.

With two working parents there wasn't enough time to make all our food from scratch. Monday night meals might be meat pies and vegetables. We would warm up six of those family pies and halve them, and have potatoes or carrots on the side. On Tuesday nights it would be dim sims and vegetables. We would steam three bags of dim sims and get six or eight each. Wednesday night was something like canned baked beans or spaghetti on toast.

I remember all this well because we had chores to do around the house, and one of mine was cooking. I often made mince stew—basically a massive pile of cheap beef mince with some onions and tinned tomatoes, and maybe a few carrots or frozen peas. Even on the nights when we ate things like dim sims, I had to prepare the vegetables to go with them. A few of my siblings would help, and we'd peel twenty potatoes and a couple of bags of carrots and just get stuck in and chop them up.

Mum often got us out of bed by 6 am to do our chores before we went to school—Dad was still asleep at this time, as he worked so late. Mum had a big chalkboard on the wall where she'd write everyone's name. It was like a military operation. And if Mum ever had to start work earlier than usual, the next in the chain of command, the oldest kid living at home at the time, took charge.

Alongside our names on that chalkboard were the jobs we had to do. Some of us would get food ready for that night's dinner while others made the school lunches. Some would be cleaning the house or putting dirty clothes in the washing machine or hanging clothes out on the line. Mum would motivate us by saying, 'If your jobs aren't done you won't be going to footy training tonight.' If there was no training that night, she would just say that if we didn't do as we were told we wouldn't be able to play footy in the street. That was enough.

When it came to education, the primary school kids went to Corpus Christi, a Catholic primary school in Glenroy. The older ones went to Box Forest Secondary College, which was just down the end of our street. No one in our family cared much about the academic side of schooling. When I was at school, I just mucked around in class until lunchtime arrived and I could go out on the oval and play footy or cricket with the boys. The only school subject I liked was physical education, because in that class we mainly went outside and played sport.

When we arrived home from school there were usually more chores to do before we could go out and kick the footy. But as soon as Mum said everything was sweet, we were off. Rain, hail or shine. On non-training nights, we would play footy in the street until Mum came out and told us to come inside. In winter, it was often pitch-black by the time she dragged us inside for dinner.

We often set up goals out the front of our house, but sometimes a big mob of us neighbourhood kids went to the local oval, which was literally at the end of our street. When it was time for dinner, if Mum couldn't find us in our street she would head straight for the oval. We weren't naughty kids. We didn't go places where Mum couldn't find us or get into fights. We just loved playing football.

On those occasions when we went up to the oval, we often played a mad and chaotic sort of no-rules match. I loved those games of footy. A few other girls, including many of my sisters, joined in with the games, but none of them loved footy as much as me.

There were some hard times during those years, like when Dad was diagnosed with leukaemia and could no longer work. Money became really tight and we had to live an even more basic life. Mum would buy a big bag of carrots and shave them down into a soup, and that's all we had to eat. Even though we hated the taste, it was food, and we knew Mum was doing the best she could. Sometimes, though, we benefitted from the generosity of others in our suburb.

The owners of the Glenroy Bakery looked after us like we were family. I can vividly remember the first time I walked past the bakery and they were making doughnuts. I was still in primary school and a few of us kids were on our way to Coles to buy some extra things for dinner. The smell from the bakery just about tripped us over. It was so good. We decided to go in and see if they would give us some and, amazingly, the person behind the counter gave us a whole bag of doughnuts. They were so fresh. The greatest thing I had ever tasted.

After that we started making a habit of sneaking down to the bakery at the end of the day to see if we could get some free doughnuts. Mum would have been horrified if she knew we were getting food without paying for it, so we didn't tell her. We either ate them before we got home or smuggled them into our bedroom. Sometimes the people at the bakery even gave us doughnuts with jam in the middle. Seriously, they were heaven. I still love them, but they don't taste as good as they used to. I think that's because I can now afford more treat food, so eating doughnuts isn't as special an experience as it once was.

My parents were both so selfless. They would go hungry if that was the only way to ensure all of us kids had enough to eat. Mum and Dad would give us the clothes off their backs if we needed them. We knew we were loved and that we were being looked after as well as our parents could manage.

Even though it was challenging at times, my parents loved having a big family. My mum, Rosemary, has Māori heritage. She is related to the renowned Māori leader Sir Graham Latimer, who was the president of the New Zealand Māori Council for more than forty years and in the 1980s led the fight to secure Māori rights, under the Treaty of Waitangi, to New Zealand's state-owned lands, forests and fisheries. Mum grew up in New Zealand, in a culture where large families are the norm. As a result, she always wanted to have lots of kids. I'm not really sure whether Dad, who had German heritage but grew up in Queensland, always wanted to have so many kids or it just happened that way.

Mum met Dad in New Zealand when she was nineteen. I'm told he was a DJ back then. He was apparently very well known in the pub scene in Melbourne at the time. I'm not sure why he went to New Zealand, but I think it must have been to do some gigs over there. After he met Mum they decided to move to Melbourne together.

Mum was Dad's second wife. He had two girls—Eleanor and Kim—with his first wife. Then he had twelve more kids with Mum. Sometimes I still struggle to name us all. I find it easiest to go through the list in birth order, from youngest to oldest, so here goes: Ethan, Livinia, Elena, Gary (nicknamed Barney), me, Bree, Melanie, Renee, Corey, Jamie, Shona and Jennifer.

The sleeping arrangements when I was a kid took some organisation. I recall Mum and Dad sharing one bedroom with the youngest kids while the other nine or ten of us would share the other bedroom. I think there were eight beds in that room. It was basically four sets of bunks. Sometimes we had to share a bed—that's just how it was.

All sorts of pranks happened in the kids' bedroom, like there was no tomorrow. The chief aim was to get each other in trouble with Mum and Dad. We would take the slats out of someone's bed, and then the person using that bed would fall through it. We would all laugh and Mum would have to come in and tell us off. Mum had to visit our room five or six times each night to tell us to be quiet and go to sleep. She was always trying to get us to remember that we needed a good night's sleep so we could work hard at school the next day, but given not many of us cared for school that wasn't an incentive to behave. All most of us wanted to do was kick a footy around or play cricket.

Our car was an old yellow Ford Falcon station wagon. There were often eight of us crammed into the main part of the car, while the rest went in the back. It was illegal but Dad didn't give a shit. He couldn't. It was the only way we could get around. Dad drove that old wagon up to Queensland a few times to see his brother Jack. He would take a couple of us kids with him each time, and I was usually one of the lucky ones who got to go. They were great trips.

I now know this was very different from the upbringing most kids in Australia had. But none of it seemed out of the ordinary to me at the time. We lived in a bubble, and what went on in that bubble was all I knew. There was never a time where I was saying, 'Oh, we're so broke' or, 'I'm sad because we're poor' or, 'We don't have anything like the other kids have'. If I had that time again, I would want exactly the same upbringing, because the way I grew up made me the person I am today.

I grew up in a family that looked at life the way I believe everyone should look at it. We didn't go around judging people. We weren't the sort who went around thinking, 'You don't look very rich' or, 'You don't look like you're wearing very expensive clothes' or, 'I need that really expensive house over there'. I think we just enjoyed life as it was. And the bond among us that was created during those years has endured, and we remain a very close and loving family to this day.

2
The loves of my life

I ENJOYED A VERY close relationship with both my parents during my pre-teen years. But Dad was my best friend, and I'm sure I was his. We were like two peas in a pod. To put it bluntly, I was his favourite child, closely followed by Livinia, my disabled sister. She is five years younger than me and was born with Moebius syndrome, a condition that means she cannot move her face properly and will forever have the developmental age of a six or seven year old.

I don't know why I was Dad's favourite. I always used to stir my brothers and sisters by saying, 'I'm the best kid in the family, that's why!' To be honest, I am the hardest working and most driven person in my family, and maybe Dad spotted that from when I was young. Whatever it was, we were soul mates.

I used to go everywhere with Dad I could. Some nights he even took me out on the road delivering pizzas. I always wanted to be by his side, and on some nights I would set up a makeshift bed next to his and sleep there. On the odd occasion that Mum had to do a night shift at the nursing home, I would curl up and sleep next to him.

He was such a kind and generous man. A testament to that was the amount of love he showed to Livinia. He never gave up on her. She basically died two or three times in the days after she was born, and he didn't give up. When the doctors said she would never walk, he didn't give up. When she became so blocked up with snot that she could have stopped breathing, he sat by her bed with one of those sucker things to keep clearing her nose. I'm sure that there were a couple of times when he pretty much had to resuscitate her. 'Vinny', as we all call her, was his princess.

Vinny went to a special school from age five or six. We had spent hours and hours using a specific frame to teach her how to walk, and Dad and I started going to her school every now and then to have a picnic with her and her schoolmates. Dad would break our family budget and buy lamingtons, lollies, cakes, chocolates and party pies and then walk into the school carrying all this stuff in a big basket. The kids greeted him like he was Santa Claus. Dad would spread the food out on a table and all the kids would come and have a feast. They seriously used to go nuts when he arrived. They loved him. 'Gary's here!' they would shout. They would jump on him and he enjoyed every minute of it.

It was Dad who sparked my passion for football. He was a big Essendon man, and he absolutely loved footy. He would happily watch footy all day, whether it was live at a footy ground or on television, or a replay. Although we were amazingly close, we didn't barrack for the same AFL team. He and the rest of my family lived for the Bombers, but I barracked for Hawthorn. When I was about four or five years old, I had discovered our next-door neighbour barracked for the Hawks. He was a really good footy player, and I wanted to be like him, so I went for Hawthorn too. I don't think Dad was very happy with my decision, but given the rest of the family followed his lead and supported Essendon, I don't think he had much to complain about.

We all loved watching the AFL on the TV, but in our household playing footy was a bigger thing than watching it. My older brothers started out playing for the Hadfield Football Club in the Essendon District league. Hadfield is the neighbouring suburb to where we lived in Glenroy, so Dad and I often went down there to watch. I loved watching the boys play, and I was rapt that Hadfield players wore Hawthorn-style brown and gold stripes and the team was known as the Hawks. But I was just so frustrated as well, because I wanted to be out on the field. As soon as each quarter finished, I headed straight onto the ground, kicking a footy of my own.

At the start, I loved footy because Dad loved it, but I soon developed my own passion for the game. Mum remembers that by the age of three I carried a footy with me wherever I went. I even took it to bed every night. I was already very competitive. When I watched my brothers playing proper games of footy, I wanted to do the same.

Right from the start, Dad encouraged me to play sport, especially the sports that didn't usually attract a lot of female players. He never once said anything like, 'Girls can't be playing footy' or, 'Girls are no good at cricket'. He was far more likely to say, 'You can be whatever you want to be. If playing cricket is what you want to do, I'll support it.' Dad wasn't only happy for me to play male-dominated sports, he was adamant that I could be better than the boys.

'You need to beat them,' he would tell me.

When I was at the footy oval or out in the street, I loved trying to kick the ball further than my brothers did. I imagined that I was one of my Hawthorn heroes: Dermott Brereton or Jason Dunstall or John Platten or Chris Langford or Daniel Harford or Shane Crawford. They could all kick the ball so far. I remember in the early days I couldn't even kick the length of the goal square, but Dad encouraged me to get better and better. When I was old enough, he became like my personal coach. He would take me down to the local oval and get me to work on my fitness and my skills. I don't think he had been much of a footy player in his day, but he was a great teacher. The kicking skills that hold me in such good stead today are a product of his brilliant teaching.

Mum and I have recently talked a lot about this time. We started doing so when we were asked to be part of an episode about women's footy for the ABC show *Australian Story*. And we have reminisced some more since I started writing this book.

'You used to go out there and kick the ball, and then Dad would take you for a lap of the oval,' Mum told me. 'You would spend endless hours outside kicking the footy and running around.'

By the age of six, I was itching to play a proper game of footy. Hadfield had a number of junior teams and I was adamant that I was good enough to hold my own. I started going to training when I was six, even though I think the league's rules stated that I couldn't play a game until I turned seven. I was able to compete so well with the boys on the training track that when my seventh birthday arrived I went straight into the team—and I was the only girl in the side.

Dad was extremely proud when he saw me run onto the field in Hadfield's brown and gold stripes. Before the game, he had given me just one piece of advice: 'If you want to play with the boys you have to take the hits.' He had nothing to worry about in that regard. I was so looking forward to playing and that meant taking some hits and dishing plenty out as well, just like it did when I was playing against my brothers in our backyard.

From that first game, my competitiveness kicked in and I revelled in the challenge of trying to be the best player on the field. I loved it when the boys tried to tackle me and I was able to get around them because I was so fast and agile. Dad loved that too. He started calling me 'Mouse', because I was clearly the smallest player on the field. But I often heard him cheering and laughing as I dodged around boys that were twice my size. I was so short that sometimes it looked like I was running through their legs.

There were times when the boys caught me and threw me to the ground. But I took the blows, clambered back on my feet, and got on with the game. Dad thought I was the toughest player at the club, and he never once questioned whether it was right for a girl to be playing a sport that can be so rough.

I was never one for analysing this unusual situation either. For me, playing footy was never about trying to prove a point that girls could hold their own against boys, or anything like that. I just loved footy, so that's why I played it. It was the same with cricket. I played it because I loved it. And when I was at training or playing in a match, I just felt like I was one of the boys. To be honest, it never crossed my mind that I was any different from them.

I didn't read newspapers or magazines or watch television shows that promoted the idea that girls should do this and boys should do that. It never really crossed my mind that some people might have thought a girl playing footy against boys was a bit weird. When

I think about today's kids, there are so many influences that can screw them up. They look at magazines full of pretty girls and think, 'That's what I need to look like. I need to be a princess.' And the boys see pictures of buffed Adonises—it's all bullshit.

Recently I have read so many stories about how it's controversial that girls want to have a kick with the boys. Those stories are so harmful. We should just let our kids explore their interests and encourage them. If a young boy wants to be a ballet dancer, let him be a ballet dancer—don't tell boys that they can't be ballet dancers. If the kids want to play soccer, let them play soccer. Don't preach to your kids, 'Oh, it's so weird to see a girl playing football' or, 'Boys don't do ballet'. Be careful what you say, because we all know that kids soak up what their parents say and then go and repeat many of the things they hear. A young girl who wants to play footy doesn't need some boy coming up to her and saying it's not what girls do.

The boys I played cricket and footy alongside and against were fantastic. I can't remember one ever saying, 'You're a girl, you can't kick' or, 'You're a girl, you shouldn't be playing'. When I played cricket, the boys bowled as fast at me as they did at any other batsman. To be fair, I then bowled just as fast at them. Those kids were never judgemental, and that's why I feel children are the best people to be around if they have not had their heads filled with prejudices.

One of the things I love the most about playing sport is being part of a team. Right from those years when I was just a little tacker, being in a team felt like being part of another big family. Whether it was footy or cricket, we were all in it together. My brother Barney, who is just one year younger than me, and I were often on the same team. He is my closest sibling—in age and in terms of being friends—and we both lived for sport back then. Our lives were about cricket in the cricket season and footy in the footy season. That's pretty much all we cared about.

I played in the Hadfield footy club's junior boys teams until I was twelve. I was a little midfielder who loved to run forward and kick goals. Without wanting to sound like a big-head, I was better than most of the boys. I regularly won best-on-ground awards after games and I was right up there in the best and fairest at the end of each season. I was able to give my brothers a lot of shit, as I usually came home from the end-of-season function carrying a bag full of awards, while they came home with nothing. It made me feel like I was Number One in our household.

I'm not one for remembering every minor detail, but I think I played in at least one premiership as a child. The thing was that winning or losing wasn't a big part of footy at that age. If we didn't win, we didn't all walk around scowling and saying, 'We lost'. For us, footy was just about having fun with our mates. One of the highlights for me each week was getting a free can of soft drink and some lollies after the game. The people at the Hadfield Football Club were so lovely to my brothers and me. They knew our family didn't have much money, so they would often give us a free hot dog or pie, and that was like heaven. They were great days. You got to play with some of your best mates and you got a free hot dog and a drink. That's what sport should be all about for kids. It's not about winning or losing or how many goals you kicked. It's about being part of a fun environment and trying your hardest.

Those days continued until my gender inevitably came into play. The rules of our local footy competition stated that girls could only play against boys until they turned thirteen. So when I reached my teens I switched across to Hadfield's open-age women's team—the club didn't have any junior teams for girls. Although I weighed no more than 40 kilograms, I was soon lining up against fully grown, big-bodied women. The only special rule put in place for me was that I had to wear a helmet.

Thanks to my apprenticeship against the boys, I was soon running rings around my opposition, and getting in a few fracas with them, as my great friend Nicole Graves, who was playing for the Darebin Falcons at the time, says:

> I played against Mo when I was nineteen or twenty and she would have been only twelve or thirteen. You know, there were quite a few twelve year olds playing open-age women's footy then, because there was nowhere else for them to play. She was so tiny that I was worried I was going to squish her, but then she kept turning our defenders inside out and kicked five goals in half a game. She started getting a bit cocky, so I said to her, 'Who do you think you are, you little shit?' She sledged me straight back, then we went our separate ways and nothing else came of it. All these years later, we still joke about it.

When I was thirteen, in 2001, I helped the Hadfield Hawks win the Division 2 premiership in the VWFL. Our victory resulted in us being promoted to Division 1. Playing against the top women's teams in Victoria was something that I was really excited about and looking forward to—it was a dream come true. However, the 2002 season would coincide with the toughest period of my life.

3

No better man

IT WAS WHEN I was eleven years old that my dad was diagnosed with leukaemia. Initially, I had no real idea about how serious his illness was. When I was told that he had cancer, I was like, whatever. I had no idea what cancer was. I didn't know there were different types of cancer. I thought he just had something like the flu. I remember people at school saying that cancer was really bad. But I thought it was impossible that a disease could kill someone as strong as my dad. He was a massive man. I think he weighed about 140 kilograms, but he wasn't fat. He was quite tall and was built like a big rugby player. When I looked at him, I couldn't see how an illness could possibly be stronger than him.

Even after the high doses of chemotherapy that Dad was receiving resulted in him losing his hair, I still didn't think much about it. I always thought he'd be better in a couple more weeks. But over the course of two years Dad's health deteriorated to the point where he was unable to drive, then unable to even walk, and it was then that the extent of how sick he was dawned on me.

Eventually, it got to the point where Dad was unable to cope with all the noise and chaos at home. The doctors were adamant that being around his family was proving very stressful for Dad. As he wasn't one to complain, Mum took it upon herself to rent a small unit for him. I couldn't bear being away from Dad at night, so I decided that I was going to be his carer. I didn't ask Mum whether I could do it, I just told her I was going to look after him. I had to be there for him, and that was that.

I ended up caring for Dad for more than two years. I made all his food and I took care of all the medical things that I could handle. Looking back now, I'm not really sure how I managed to look after him as well as I did, because he needed a lot of help. As his illness progressed, he started coughing up a lot of blood. He would cough into a spit bag and I would change the bag every couple of hours. I was by his side right through the night. In fact, I don't think I ever had a full night's sleep during those years.

I missed a lot of school during the period that I was caring for Dad, but I don't remember my teachers trying to stop me from being by his side. I think they understood how close I was to him. I think they also knew that Dad pretty much needed full-time care but Mum couldn't provide it because she had to keep working to support our huge family. She was now our sole income earner. Without her bringing in money, we wouldn't have been able to pay our bills or the two rents. We would have been homeless. If Mum had a weekday off or did a nightshift, then she looked after Dad during the day while I went to school. That's how it worked.

In his last year or so, Dad was often admitted to hospital. He sometimes developed pneumonia and he needed blood transfusions. He always went to St Vincent's hospital in Fitzroy and I always went with him. We travelled there by taxi until Dad was so sick that we had to go by ambulance. When he was getting transfusions and stuff like that, I had no idea what was going on or why he needed new blood. But I never left his side. If he had to stay overnight, I pushed two chairs together and slept beside him. The nurses became so used to me doing this that they started setting up a bed for me on the floor. I never left him while he was in hospital, and Dad always shared his food with me. We were there for each other.

Towards the end of his life, Dad became very fragile. On one occasion he rolled over in bed and one of his ribs fractured. It was heartbreaking to see him reduced from such a big, strong man to a pile of skin and splintering bones. I think that he ended up weighing just 38 kilograms. He became so skinny that when I rubbed his back I could clearly see the shape of his tailbone.

When Dad got to the point where he knew he was going to die, he moved back into our family home, and I did too. Dad wanted to be surrounded by his family in his last few days, but he went through a really emotional period once we moved back home. I remember I was watching television in the lounge room with my brother Barney one evening and I could hear Mum saying to Dad, 'Don't be an idiot. Don't say things like that.' The thing was that Dad had started pouring out all of his life's regrets. Over and over again, he kept telling Mum that he had so many regrets about his life. He kept saying that he regretted working in a job that meant he didn't spend enough time with his kids. And he was crying a lot. That was a massive shock for me. I don't think I had ever seen him cry before then.

Dad knew he was about to die, and he was just going through that phase of full-blown regret. He was thinking, Fuck, why didn't I just do things that I wanted to do? Why did I go waste all that time working nightshifts? So many things must have been going through his head. I remember he called one of my older siblings into his bedroom and started apologising to them. He couldn't stop saying, 'I'm sorry.'

Mum kept telling him to stop saying these things, to stop feeling like he needed to apologise to everyone. But Dad just couldn't help it. He couldn't find any inner peace. I had no idea what was going on. Deep down, I still didn't believe he was going to die. I just didn't want to believe it.

It was 2002, I was fourteen and enrolled in Box Forest Secondary College (which was closed down at the end of 2009 and then reopened as Glenroy College). I was doing what was known as the Koorie Open Door Education (KODE) program, which meant I was in classes with kids—most of them Indigenous—who needed extra help with their reading and writing, which I did too. People probably judged me for being in the program. They probably thought it meant I was dumb. But I didn't give a shit. I loved it. I found a certain amount of freedom being with others who struggled academically.

Even though I was missing a lot of school days because of Dad's illness, the teachers wanted me to take part in the work experience program. Dad thought it would be good for me too. He wanted me to be someone who grew up and made a contribution to society, not someone who turned into a dole bludger. So my school arranged for me to spend a week at the local Bi-Lo supermarket. It was the one where we did most of our shopping and where two of my sisters already worked. But I didn't want to go. The day before I was due to start, Dad called me over and quietly said, 'Hey, you have to go to work experience. Your school has set it up, so you have to go.'

'Fuck that, I'm not going,' I replied. 'I have to be here with you.'

But Dad was adamant.

'You have to go.'

The next day I went down to Bi-Lo and followed my sisters around. One of them was a duty supervisor and the other one was basically a full-time shelf stacker. The following morning I got up and went to see Dad. He looked unbelievably weak, and it was soon decided that he would need to be admitted to hospital.

'I'm coming with you,' I said. He then plucked up the strength to say, 'No. You have to go to work experience. You're not coming.'

I started crying and lost it.

'Fuck this, I hate this,' I yelled. 'Fuck work experience, who cares about work experience?'

He looked at me and repeated what he had said earlier: 'You have to go.'

At 11 am, as I wandered around the supermarket, one of the staff members came up to me and said, 'Your mum has just rung. You have to go home.' I thought that Mum must have organised for us to go and see Dad at the hospital. When I got home, she asked us to sit down in the lounge room. All of my brothers and sisters were there.

'Your father might pass away soon,' she said. It was like a hit across the head and I think I started going into shock. I felt so numb. Then the phone rang and Mum answered it. I'll never forget seeing her drop to her knees, like she was sort of fainting. She started crying hysterically. One of my brothers could tell that I wasn't really registering what was going on.

'Dad has died,' he said.

Those words struck me hard. I had been by his side day after day and now he had passed away while I was at a stupid supermarket doing work experience. I felt so bitter. My best friend, my only really close friend, was gone and I had not been there at the end. To this day, the thought of Dad dying in that hospital without his family makes me cry. It breaks my heart. I went with him every time he went to the hospital, but on the one day that I didn't go with him he died.

But it was probably a very selfless act for Dad to push me away that day. He knew how close he was to dying and for a young kid like me to watch a parent die would be extremely traumatic—probably more traumatic than not being there. So in some ways I'm grateful for what he did.

I found it impossible to process the idea that Dad was gone forever. I remember family friends saying to me, 'I'm so sorry to hear about your dad,' but I sort of acted like I didn't know what they were talking about. On one level, it just didn't feel real. A carload of my teammates from the Hadfield footy club came over to see me, which was really sweet. One of them suggested, 'Let's go and play basketball to take your mind off things.' I was rapt to get the chance to go out and play some sport, but I was in a state where my mind didn't really need to be diverted. It hadn't fully registered the gravity of what had happened. Even after being given the chance to go to the funeral home and view his body in the casket, I still couldn't really grasp the reality. I had seen him lying there, clearly lifeless, but I couldn't stop believing that somehow it was just a bad dream.

I didn't really take it in at the time, but a freakish thing happened at Dad's funeral. He had chosen the song 'Better Man' by Robbie Williams for the service. But when the time came for the song to be played, the next track, which was 'My Way', came on instead. I love to think that Dad changed his mind up in heaven and reached down into the church and changed the track, because 'My Way' was so much more appropriate. Dad used to do everything his way; it was his way or the highway. Nobody ever overruled him. He was the one to have the first and last say in everything.

After the church service, the people who ran the funeral home were really apologetic about the mix-up with the music. They kept saying things like, 'We put it on Track 1, we don't know how it got to Track 2.' I know people will probably think I'm crazy saying this, but I'm sure Dad did it.

Another strange thing happened not long after the funeral. Mum was sitting on her bed crying with a few of us trying to comfort her when Livinia walked in. Vinny was the only one who didn't see Dad's casket, because she genuinely wasn't able to process what had happened. She really thought that Dad had just gone down to the shops and would return home soon. But she came into Mum's room and pronounced, 'I saw Dad last night.' Then she said it again. I started trying to distract Vinny, because I thought what she was saying would make Mum even more emotional. But Vinny kept talking.

'Yeah,' she went on, 'Dad was wearing his brown leather jacket, his blue pants and his favourite shoes.' Mum sat up and said, 'What did you say?' Vinny was describing the outfit that Dad was dressed in as he lay there in his coffin. Then Vinny looked at Mum and said, 'You know who else was there?' She then told us a name, which I have now forgotten, but let's say it was 'John Smith'. The next time we went to the cemetery, we saw that a John Smith was buried next to Dad. It was bizarre. It was like Dad had planted a dream in Vinny's brain.

Mum struggled to come to terms with her loss for a long time after Dad died. She cried and cried and cried. I think she made matters worse by playing the CD made for the funeral over and over again. The songs 'Better Man' and 'My Way' seemed to make her more emotional but she kept pressing repeat and listening to them again and again. Some days Mum struggled to even get out of bed. Watching Mum in that state, with tears continually pouring down her cheeks, was unbelievably tough. She was, and is, such an amazingly strong woman, but I think she felt scared to be on her own with so many kids to support. None of us knew what to do to help her. We tried to by sitting on her bed and gathering around her. Six or seven of us would give her group hugs. But, really, I struggled to grasp exactly why she was so sad at the time, because I had shut out the enormity of what had happened. It wasn't until many years later that the loss of my dad properly sank in.

I eventually went back to school full time. Missing so much schooling during those years that Dad was sick had put me well behind my classmates, and I never caught up. But I didn't care then and I don't care now. If somebody says to me, 'I can turn back time and if you go to school instead of looking after your dad you'll end up being the prime minister and earning one million dollars a year,' I would reply, 'No thanks.'

I am proud to have lived my life the way I want to live it. I have never forgotten Dad having all those regrets on his deathbed. Never, ever do I want to be that person. I don't want to get to the end of my life and wish that I'd done things differently. I cared for Dad because I loved him. Our life was not about money or having a big house or a big TV or the latest mobile phone. We didn't have any of that, but we had the most priceless thing in the world, and that's love. I loved my dad and that's why I made so many sacrifices for him. I wouldn't change that aspect of my life for anything. The only thing I would change, if I could, is to be by Dad's side on the day he died.

4
Sport on my mind

MY DISTRACTION FROM the grief of losing my dad was sport. Because he had encouraged me to play footy and cricket, sport was also my connection to memories of him. When I was out on the footy field or playing cricket it felt like he was there by my side.

The people at the Hadfield footy club were like another family to me at this time. They had supported me so much when my dad died—a few carloads of them came to his funeral, which is something I will treasure forever—and they were always looking out for me. It was through this period that I became really close friends with someone in the women's team, Emily Woods. She had spent a bit of time around the club during the 2001 season and then decided to have a real crack at playing footy in 2002. I was a bit shy around her at the start, but she soon took me under her wing and became like a big sister to me. She was always there when I needed a lift somewhere or just needed someone to talk to. Emily, who is six years older than me, is one of the most amazing and generous people I have ever met.

She has a much better memory for details than I do and this is how, she tells me, we came to know each other:

> I remember going out and watching Hadfield in their Division 2 Grand Final and seeing Mo, as a tiny thirteen year old, just kicking high goals from the boundary with apparent ease. I thought, 'Wow, who's this kid?' She was a very good player. But the thing that struck me once I decided to play for Hadfield the following year was that she just didn't talk. She didn't talk at all. She was so shy.
>
> But once she got to know me she really opened up and we became great friends. I always used to call her my little sister. I'm the youngest in my family, so I never had any younger sisters or brothers. Once I got to know her and her background, it was clear that she was living a somewhat troubled and difficult life, so I started sort of looking out for her. Her dad had been the one who transported her around a lot to various sporting commitments, but with him gone it became really tough. Her mum was a bit busy with all the other kids, so she was never able to help Mo get to footy games or training sessions that required travel. That's where I tried to help out as much as I could.
>
> As Mo freely admits, she wouldn't have been able to get far in her sporting career without the support of others, because she wouldn't have been able to get anywhere. But a lot of us who played footy with her could see that she had so much talent and skill. It would have been a terrible waste

> if she had been forced to give up on sport because she was unable to travel anywhere, and that's a major reason why a lot of us made a big effort to support her in that way. Even with stuff like the fees she had to pay to play footy or cricket, everyone would get around her and chip in. We just sort of did what we could for her. I remember Mo avoiding school a lot, but I tried to get her there when I could.

◆◆◆

Most of the players in our Hadfield team were out of their depth when we played our first season in Division 1 in 2002. Not only did we not win a game, we got beaten by between twenty and thirty goals pretty much every week. Emily and I and a couple of others were the only players on our side who were up to Division 1 standard. This meant that the only way we could score was to just kick the ball to each other, as Emily also recalls:

> We didn't have the greatest team, and I remember how we would kick the ball to each other. One of us would mark it and the other one would keep running so that they were the next option, and she'd mark it and I'd keep running. But she'd always make sure that she was the one that marked it in the forward fifty so that she could have the shot on goal.

In one of those seasons that I played in Hadfield's women's team I celebrated my 100th game with the club. The tally included all the games I had played with the boys in the juniors. They made a big banner for me to run through, which I was super excited about. The whole thing made me feel like the Hadfield footy community had a lot of love and respect for me, and I have no doubt that my feelings were right. They were fantastic people and they helped me so much that I will be forever grateful.

Despite losing every week by a hundred points or more during the 2002 season, our Hadfield women's team was allowed to stay in Division 1 for 2003. Once again, we copped some serious thrashings, but we did have one awesome afternoon when we defeated the Darebin Falcons in the second-last home-and-away round. I was involved in a funny incident. Before the game, our coach had given me a talking to about hogging the ball, particularly in the forward line. In my defence, getting the ball and trying to keep it was ingrained in me. When I played footy in our backyard with my brothers, it was all about getting the ball, then trying to run as fast as you could and booting it through the makeshift goals we set up. When I started out in Hadfield's women's team that's how I played. I just tried to get the ball, run as far as I could, then kick a goal. I used to try to run around everyone, then boot the crap out of the ball. I didn't know any other way to play, which meant it took the coaches at Hadfield a long time to get me to understand that sticking to our game plan and sharing the ball around could actually help the team.

That day I ran onto the field adamant I was going to do what the coach asked and share the ball around more. When the game was on the line in the last quarter, with only a few points separating us and the Falcons, I received the ball deep in the forward line and started running towards the goal square. I could have taken two more steps, steadied, then easily kicked the goal, but I suddenly remembered what the coach had said. Oh crap, I thought. He's going to think I'm being selfish if I kick the goal. So I stopped and turned around, then fired off a handball to a shocked teammate. She pulled herself together and kicked the goal, but our runner then came straight out to me with a message from the coach.

'If you're 5 metres out from goal you just put it through,' she said. 'We want you to share the ball but we don't want you to cost us the game!' In the end, we did win the game, which meant my antics created much laughter during our raucous post-match celebrations.

That same year, Emily and I were lucky enough to be selected for a City versus Country women's match, which was used to help select the Victorian squad to play in the AFL Women's National Championships. The Country team was a bit short on numbers, so I was a country girl for the day and ended up playing against Emily, who was part of the City team. We were the only Hadfield players to take part, and there was a big picture of us in the local paper, which was pretty cool. I can't remember who won the game, but neither of us made it into the Victorian squad.

Hadfield ended up being relegated back to Division 2 after the 2003 season. It soon became clear to Emily and me that we needed to keep playing in Division 1 if we wanted to have any chance of playing for Victoria at the 2004 national championships. Emily, who was working in a music store in the city at the time, knew some girls playing out at the Eastern Devils, so we ended up moving to their club.

I liked the idea of playing for the Devils, but they were based out in East Burwood in Melbourne's eastern suburbs, a long way from my place in Glenroy. However, Emily offered to drive me to training each week—often a two-hour round trip—and then take me to the games, which was an amazing gesture.

Given the Devils were based in the eastern suburbs, where the people with money live, I felt a bit out of place, rocking up in my cheap clothes. They all wore nice new runners and clothes made by the big brand names. I was most jealous of the girls who wore Nike gear. I don't really know why, but I was obsessed with Nike stuff. I just loved the swoosh logo and I loved the great athletes, like the famous sprinter Michael Johnson and the great basketballer Michael Jordan, who were part of the Nike family. I wanted to have my own Nike gear, so I started using a Texta to draw the swoosh on the cheap t-shirts and shorts that Mum bought me from Kmart or Target.

I can't draw for shit, so I'm sure the swoosh looked like a scribbled line, but I thought it looked legit. One time, during the summer, I bought a headband and drew the swoosh on it, and then wore it to cricket training. My mates were like, 'Hey, did you draw that on it?' I was like, 'Nah, I bought it.' They probably laughed at me, but I didn't care.

During my one season with the Devils, I had to be a different player than I had been at Hadfield, as Emily remembers only too well:

> I think she probably had to adapt to the fact that it was a better team, so she wasn't the star. The Devils had better coaching and there was a bit more structure to our game plan, so everyone had a bit of a role to play. This was when Mo started playing in the forward line, as the Devils already had a lot of good midfielders. She played across half-forward and stuck to her role reasonably well, although she was always trying to snag a goal!

Playing as a half-forward didn't stop me from making an impression on the state selectors, and I lived out one of my sporting dreams when I was picked to be in the Victorian squad that played at the AFL Women's National Championships in Adelaide. At just sixteen, I was one of the youngest members of the squad. Raising the money to go on the trip was a challenge, but the VWFL helped everyone in the squad by holding auction nights and things like that. Each player still had to cover a gap in the funding, but the people at the Devils rallied around and covered it for me.

Being so shy made the trip very daunting for me, as did the idea of travelling so far from home. But there were four other Devils players in the squad, so that made it a lot easier. I'm not sure I could have plucked up the courage to go if they hadn't been on the trip. In the end, it all worked out. We won the tournament and I played pretty well, getting a few mentions of being among our best players.

Although my career was on the up and I really enjoyed playing for the Devils, I felt like I was putting a lot of strain on Emily. She was using up so much of her time driving over to Glenroy to pick me up. Emily was great about it, but I didn't want to become a burden to her. Just as I was thinking that I needed to find a club closer to home, Emily told me that she was moving to Adelaide for work. For a while, I felt like the rug had been pulled out from underneath me. I really relied on her for a lot of support. But I came to the conclusion that everything would be okay if I just started playing footy in my own neck of the woods.

Everything did fall into place when Nicole Graves, who was now the president of the Darebin Falcons, asked me to come and play for the Falcons. The club is based in the suburb of Preston, just 10 kilometres east of my family home. Nicole knew I came from a family who didn't have much money, so she generously said that she would cover my fees if I wanted to play for the Falcons. I signed up straightaway.

I arrived at the Falcons in 2005, at a time when the club was about to take the VWFL by storm. Under the coaching of Peta Searle, who has gone on to become a development coach at St Kilda, the Falcons would win five successive premierships between 2006 and 2010, and I would be lucky enough to feature in the first four of them. In 2005, however, we made the Grand Final but were beaten by Melbourne University. Still, that loss didn't take the gloss off what was a great season for me.

That year Victoria fielded a second team in the AFL Women's National Championships, which were played in Melbourne. There was a very good reason for the change: the Vics had won every Grand Final since the championships were first held in 1992. The extra Victorian team was made up of players aged nineteen and under. Not only was I selected to play in the new team, I was also made captain.

Our squad was made up of young girls and we were outsized by the adult women playing in the other teams, but we had some serious talent in our line-up. We played really well during the round-robin matches, defeating every non-Victorian team and almost toppling the Vics' open-age side. We ended up playing the open-age Victorian team again in the Grand Final, but this time we were no match for their strength and skill. Tired after playing a number of games in the space of a week, we lost by more than a hundred points. However, my highlight of the week came after the Grand Final, when I was announced the player of the championships. To win such an award, at the age of seventeen, was an amazing buzz.

When playing for Victoria, I swapped between centre half-forward and full-forward, but when I was back at the Falcons I played most of my footy out of the goal square. It was a great position to play, as we had some superstar midfielders, like Daisy Pearce and Natalie Wood, who delivered the ball to me beautifully. They helped me top the VWFL goal-kicking table in my second, third and fourth seasons with the club. I kicked eighty goals in 2006, seventy-nine in 2007 and seventy-one in 2008. It was around this time that I started wearing number 23. You might think I chose that particular number because I loved all the great sportsmen who had worn it, like Michael Jordan, Buddy Franklin and Shane Warne. But I chose it as a tribute to my dad, who died on 23 August 2001.

During the time that I played for the Falcons, Nicole Graves became like a second mother to me, and I ended up living with her for a couple of years. Nicole recalls how it was that I came to live at her place:

> Because all of Mo's nieces and nephews were living with her mum, there was something like twenty children living in the house. Mo's mum is an amazing woman, but she was under the pump big-time. I used to pick up Mo and take her to footy training and we used to have a lot of conversations as we were driving. She was getting really upset because every time she left the house the other kids would go into her room and steal her stuff. She was worried that they were going to wreck her music collection, which was one of the most important things in her life at the time. She eventually put a padlock on her door, which was pretty crazy. I had a

free bedroom at my house, so I said to her, 'How about I have a chat to your mum and then you come and camp with me.' We had the discussion and it was agreed that she would come and live at my house.

Nicole was amazingly generous to me. She went and bought me a bed and some bedside tables. I had never had my own stuff like that before, so I felt like the luckiest person in the world.

In 2006, when I was eighteen, I was once again selected to be in the Victorian under-19 team that played at the national championships. This time Daisy Pearce was made captain. We ended up making it to the bronze medal match, but we lost to Queensland by thirty-six points. Playing full-forward, I had a great carnival and was one of five players from our team selected to be in the All Australian team. Two of my Falcons teammates, Daisy Pearce and Lauren Arnell, also made this prestigious team. Daisy and I were then granted an amazing opportunity when we were selected to be in an Australian team that travelled to Ireland to play two International Rules matches against the best female Gaelic footballers.

Nicole Graves coached the Australian team and also organised the trip, and she explains how this all came about:

> I played some Gaelic footy in Australia and was part of a couple of tours to Ireland, so I knew quite a few people at the Gaelic Athletic Association. I spoke to them about setting up a two-match International Rules tour, similar to what the AFL players had done. Women's Gaelic football was already huge in Ireland, and TG4, which is the Gaelic TV station

over there, said they would telecast the matches live. So we started fundraising and went from there.

TG4 ended up giving us $50,000 to get over there, so they were really fantastic. The AFL supplied all the uniforms, and all the girls fundraised, and in the end we spent two and a half weeks in Ireland for about $1200 each, which wasn't bad.

Despite that money from the Irish TV station and the money from fundraising, we still had to cover some of the trip costs ourselves. My mum wasn't in a position to contribute any money for me, so Nicole reached into her own pocket and paid my share herself. She is renowned for such acts of generosity. As Nicole likes to say, 'No kid in my charge doesn't go somewhere because of money.' Nicole also helped me organise a passport, which proved to be quite a saga because we couldn't find my birth certificate. To be honest, I don't know if my parents even kept any of our birth certificates. But after a few visits to the office of Births, Deaths and Marriages we managed to get it sorted.

Our 25-strong Australian squad was not only made up of the best women's Australian Rules footballers in the country, we also had a few girls who had mainly played Gaelic footy. They were a great help, as they had all the knowledge of how to kick a round ball. Daisy Pearce and I were by far the youngest members of the touring party, but the other women looked after us so well. We were like a big family.

The whole trip to Ireland was incredible. For someone who had rarely left Melbourne, travelling to the other side of the earth was an absolute head-spin. Emerging from my bubble in Glenroy into the wide world made me feel like a caged animal being let out into the jungle. I kept thinking, Oh my God, there's a whole different world out there, with people who speak funny and do strange things. I was blown away by the whole experience.

We used most of the same rules as the men did for their International Rules games, but there was one key difference: no tackling. That meant we could not physically intimidate our Irish opponents like the Aussie men had done over the years—there is no tackling in Gaelic footy, so the Irish are not used to being flattened! So Nicole had picked a lot of fast players, because the Irish are renowned for their speed.

In the first game, which was played on 31 October at Breffni Park, Cavan, we were beaten 134 to 15. We were much more competitive in the second match, which was played on 4 November at Parnell Park in Dublin. But we lost that one as well. The final score was 39 to 18. In the end, we were outclassed by an Irish team who were both too quick and too skilful for us.

Despite those lopsided scores, I look back on those games with great pride. We were a team of trailblazers, and just by making it to Ireland we demonstrated that big things were going to happen in women's football in the coming years. Nicole also recalls that trip in terms of what we needed to do to move ahead:

> The big crowds and being on TV was really exciting. The scores were pretty average, but if we had been allowed to tackle it might have been different. I guess the Ireland tour was a great step for women's footy and it showed us where we were at in terms of women's sport. Our girls thought they could play at an elite level, but we got absolutely trounced.

> We were playing a very different game. It was pretty much Gaelic football. But women's football in Ireland was miles ahead of where we were at, so I suppose the tour taught us about where we needed to get to.

◆ ◆ ◆

It took a while for me to get my feet back on the ground when I returned from that tour to Ireland. I had experienced what the big, wide world had to offer and now I was back in Glenroy. Don't get me wrong, I was rapt to be back with my family, but I suddenly wanted to get on a plane and go somewhere else. I think my brothers and sisters thought I was weird when I said things like that to them. I don't think they were particularly jealous of my trip. They just never thought about the world outside our family, so they didn't see any need to go anywhere else.

The skills I learned on that tour to Ireland set me up for a big 2007 footy season. I was once again selected to be in the Victorian under-19 team that played in the AFL Women's National Championships, which this time were held at Canberra's Manuka Oval. Daisy Pearce captained our team, and we almost pulled off the upset of the carnival when we got within five points of defeating the open-age Victorian team. Daisy and I were again named in the All Australian team.

A couple of months after the championships, I attracted one of my first mentions in the national media when *The Age* writer Martin Flanagan came to a Darebin Falcons game to write a feature story on Daisy. He included some stuff about me in the article, even drawing comparisons between my evasive skills and peripheral vision and those of Chris Judd and Peter Matera. I was very happy to receive such praise from a person who must have watched a lot of footy in his time.

I think this made a lot of people in women's footy sit up and take notice of me. Maybe it played a role in boosting my reputation as one of the best female players in the country, which led to me being made captain of a Victorian team that played in the national women's championships in the late 2000s.

The funny thing was that just as my reputation as a footballer took off, I was grappling with a decision about my sporting future. I had made state and national teams in both football and cricket, and now I was being asked to decide to concentrate on one or the other.

Although I have focussed on my footy career to this point, cricket was also a massive part of my life during my teenage years. I had honed my skills during many marathon bowling and battling sessions with my brother Barney in the nets at our local oval. Some summers we went to the nets pretty much every day. We only had shitty second-hand gear, but we loved it.

I started out playing in boys' teams for the Glenroy Cricket Club. I think I could have kept playing against the boys through my teenage years, because the rules about that in cricket weren't as strict as in footy. But once I got to a certain age I just decided that I would be better off playing against girls, so that's what I did. I moved to the Merlynston Hadfield Cricket Club, and ended up playing in their women's team under the captaincy of my great friend Emily Woods.

I fancied myself as an all-rounder, and I could certainly do a bit of damage with the bat. I would try to smash every ball I faced.

I would not block; I would never block. If somebody told me to block a ball, I'd tell them to get stuffed. When I batted, I would be charging down the wicket from the first ball I faced, because I remembered training in the nets with my brothers, and I always wanted to smack their deliveries out of the park. So there was no real technique to my batting. I couldn't hit a classical cover drive or anything like that. I just tried to smash everything over midwicket or square leg.

Although my work with the willow was good enough to win me the odd batting average, I was first and foremost a fast bowler. I loved running in and trying to bowl as fast as I could. I was a little bit erratic at times, but I had a ripper bouncer, which could intimidate even grown men in the nets. In fact, I was clocked at 132 kilometres per hour when I was part of a Victorian women's state team in my late teens.

Emily Woods has some great memories of captaining me during my early years with the Merlynston Hadfield:

> Mo was a very good fast bowler. Her batting was pretty good, but she didn't like getting out. I still remember having to take her to the tribunal one time after she went off at the umpire after being given out. She was adamant that she wasn't out and I think she said some stuff to the umpire and then smashed the stumps down. Looking back, I can't help having a bit of a laugh about it, because no one ever used to go to the tribunal in women's cricket. And she was only fifteen or sixteen and I had to take her there to face the music. I had to try and control her a bit more on the field after that.

> I remember telling her to pull her head in a little bit. But she has always had this amazingly competitive spirit. There was nothing nasty about her. She just wanted to win.
>
> To be fair, I was a bit of a competitive captain, and when I wanted to get someone out I'd always bring her on, and first ball would always have to be a bouncer to show what she could do, because she did have a bit of raw pace with the cricket ball. She couldn't really control the ball as much as I would have liked, but her bouncer was good enough to scare people and put them on their back foot.

I was selected in state teams in a number of age groups and played alongside a number of girls who went on and made the Australian team, like Jess Cameron and Elyse Villani. The people from Cricket Victoria, particularly a lady called Claudia Fatone, really supported me. They were amazing. Claudia knew I was from a family who didn't have much. After all, everyone else would rock up at practice with a cricket bag full of top-notch gear, including proper cricket shoes with spikes. But I would just turn up wearing a daggy Kmart t-shirt and some cheap runners. Not that I gave a shit. I would have happily played in a pair of thongs. But when I was about fifteen, Claudia went to the Kookaburra cricket gear company and asked if they would sponsor me. The first I heard about it was when Claudia came up to me at training one day and said, 'Mo, I've got some stuff for you.' She then handed me a new cricket bag full of new gear, including shoes with spikes. I was like a kid in a candy shop. I couldn't believe it. I think I just looked at the bag and said, 'Oh my God' about fifty times. That kind of generosity means so much to someone like me, someone who has come from a family who had so little in terms of money. I treasured that cricket gear.

I was lucky enough to travel around Australia with the various state cricket teams that I played in. We went to Perth for one tournament, and that was probably the first time I went on a plane, which was pretty exciting. We also had a trip to Adelaide one year. Even going to play in Geelong was exciting for me. I was happy to go anywhere. All these places seemed exotic compared with Glenroy.

But when I reached my late teens, if I wanted to try to play open-age cricket for Australia, I was going to have to devote myself to the sport, which meant giving up footy. In a way, it was a tough call. I really wanted to try to make the Australian cricket team and play footy too. But the cricket people insisted I choose. Football was my first love, so I chose to give up on my cricket career and focus on footy.

It was sad to walk away from cricket, particularly all the mates I had made in the various state teams, but the reality is that I thought of cricket as more of an individual sport. And it's also a sport in which you can field all day and then, when you finally get a chance to bat, you can go out on the first ball. In contrast, footy is a real team game, and you get plenty of chances to make up for your mistakes. For me, playing footy was also about staying close to the memories of my dad. So it was never really a true choice between the two. I was always going to stick with footy when push came to shove.

5
Hitting rock bottom

During those teenage years, when my sporting career took off, I did try to get to school as much as I could, even though I wasn't really interested. It was hard. Box Forest Secondary College was pretty rough, but I didn't mind that. I wasn't there for any sort of academic advancement. I just went to school so that I could find some new people to kick the footy with.

I had heaps of fun in the Koorie Open Door Education program. I felt like I had come from the same upbringing as the Koori kids, in that they didn't have much and I didn't have much. So we didn't see each other as being different. And we did our best to support each other. Some of them would come to school without any lunch, because their home lives were so chaotic and their parents were either poor or wasted their money. But nobody gave a shit about that. We would simply share our food with those kids who had none. We considered ourselves among equals.

The teachers at KODE were great. Their classes were not too hard and not boring. They were chilled and they let us have a lot of fun. I was just obsessed with sport, so my favourite teacher was the sports teacher. He encouraged me to take sport a little more seriously, as he could see that I had the talent to potentially make a career out of it. And he loved seeing me out there on the field, playing cricket or footy with the boys at recess and lunchtime. I was the only girl who played sport with the boys, and those boys loved me like a brother. It was such a cool time in my life.

KODE only offered classes up to Year 10, so I transferred into the mainstream part of Box Forest Secondary College for Year 11. I didn't have anywhere near the academic skills needed to pass the Victorian Certificate of Education (VCE), so I was enrolled in the Victorian Certificate of Applied Learning (VCAL), which aims to teach students basic numeracy and literacy but also to set them up for their working lives by giving them practical work-related experience. Even so, the VCAL program was too much for me. I just didn't like being at school, learning stuff I didn't care about, so halfway through the year I quit.

At this time I was living with Nicole Graves, and I was very lucky to have her support. She helped me enrol with a job network, which got me into traffic management, the line of work I remain in today. Soon I was driving around Melbourne setting up witches hats and directing traffic around worksites. I enjoyed it, as I loved being out and about and doing stuff. Nicole made sure I was out of bed at 6 am every day so that I was at work on time. I really can't thank her enough for what she did for me.

At eighteen years old, I felt much older. I had already been through a lot in my life. I think that when people go through the kind of loss that I did, they express their feelings in a different way. I found myself desperately searching for ways to connect with Dad beyond football, because without him I often felt like I had lost everything. I no longer had my best friend to turn to. I started to think about all the great things I did with my dad and how he loved calling me Mouse. Then I had an idea: I'm going to get a tattoo of a mouse. So I did. It was my first tattoo—the first of many.

From that point on, I felt the need to express myself through body art. I didn't care whether other people thought tattoos were bogan or feral or unladylike. Expressing myself that way was what I wanted to do. I truly believe that you only live one life, and I truly believe that you are put on this earth to live how you want to live. This was another time when I thought to myself, I don't want to be on my deathbed wishing I'd done things differently, like my dad had. And the more I started to deal with my dad's death, the more art I wanted to put on my body. I had my dad's name tattooed on me, and then I added my mum's name, and also Livinia's.

Now my arms and legs are covered in wonderfully varied images, including replicas of several Salvador Dali works. I just love his paintings. They are so out there. To be able to carry them around with me every day is really special. I also have the name of a dearly departed friend tattooed in Hindi on my neck. That friend looked after me a lot when I was growing up. My body art is also about tapping into my Māori heritage. I have our tribal tattoo just above my stomach.

No one in my family has ever had a problem with my tattoos, but I couldn't say the same thing about the people who ran women's football in the mid 2000s. When I was made captain of the first Victorian under-19 team that played at the national championships in Melbourne in 2005 I tried to be a good leader, to be there for my teammates. And given we made it all the way to the Grand Final, I felt like I had done pretty well. I don't think our team would have played so well if the players had thought their captain was no good.

It was in the year between the 2005 and 2006 national championships that I got the first of my tattoos and cut my hair short. In hindsight it doesn't seem like a coincidence that they took the captaincy from me back then and gave it to Daisy Pearce, a player who had the ponytail and nice smile that the women's footy administrators seemed obsessed with at the time. They didn't even select me to be in the leadership group. For a while, I chose to ignore what had happened. I thought, Oh they're just sharing it around. Shit happens. I'll get on with playing good footy. But I soon became convinced that the reason they took the captaincy from me was my short hair and tattoos, and I remain certain about that to this day.

A lot of people thought that everyone who played women's footy was a lesbian. Sure, there were some gay girls among the various teams that were part of the VWFL, but there were plenty of others, like Daisy Pearce and myself, who were not—and are not. The administrators were paranoid about the perception that women's footy was full of tattooed, butch dykes. They believed that to succeed women's football had to appeal to men, and they didn't think that blokes liked this kind of woman. They were just hoodwinking themselves into believing that they had to sex up women's footy to be what they thought men wanted.

In the process of doing that, it felt to players like me that they wanted to stop everyone from just being themselves, and were sidelining those who did not fit the image of clean-cut, ponytailed girls they were trying to promote. When I got my hair cut short and embraced the world of body art, it felt to me that they thought people would assume I was a heavy-duty lesbian, as if sexuality somehow had a bearing on whether you were good at what you did or not, or whether you were a good person or not. Although they wanted me to keep playing—I was one of the best players in the state, after all—they didn't seem to want me to hold a leadership role or be part of the push to promote the women's game. This really left a huge negative mark on me, making me wonder where I stood in all this, even while I thought their stance was pathetic and undersold our skills and commitment.

It made me doubt whether the people running the game I loved wanted me to succeed. I felt like they were becoming more and more judgemental as I added tattoos to my body as a means of self-expression. The way they treated me was so different from the way the girls my age treated each other at the footy club. Some of those girls had short hair and some of them didn't, but we never assumed things like, 'She's got short hair, she must be gay.' It was only the 'adults' who worried about this stuff. When I mucked around with kids my own age, we never had those sorts of conversations. The conversations we had were like, 'What's the latest song, so I can put it on my iPod?' or, 'Who's got the playlist today?' or, 'Let's win today.'

I played in the national championships again in 2007 and 2008, in the open-age team, and I tried to enjoy myself. I was old enough to drink legally—although most kids who grow up in Glenroy start drinking a few years before they turn eighteen—and that meant those footy carnivals were like one big party. You would wake up in the morning, go play a game of footy, have some food and a brief rest, play another game, then head to a bar with the players from all the other teams and get drunk. We barely did any kind of warm-up before the matches, and there were no recovery sessions or ice baths afterwards. We didn't have any staff telling us what to eat or keeping our fitness on track. There was just one coach and one trainer, who strapped ankles and gave rubdowns. Those carnivals were just about playing footy and getting hammered. Which felt great at the time!

I also achieved a lot in club football in 2006, 2007 and 2008. I played in three premierships with Darebin and topped the VWFL goal-kicking table each year. But in 2009 I got the telephone call that set me back big time. When the VWFL asked me to cover up my tattoos for the *Herald Sun* photo shoot, I really started to wonder why people were being so judgemental about me. So many thoughts coursed through my brain about what I could have done wrong to end up here. They had taken the under-19 team captaincy from me back in 2006 and now they were overtly telling me to change who I was.

The whole saga really got me down, but I kept playing and was part of the Falcons' 2009 Grand Final win. My role in this success—and the three previous flags—would see me feature in the Falcons' Silver Jubilee Team, which was picked in 2015, to mark the 25th anniversary of the club's founding:

Backs: Patricia Kinnersly, Roi Boutsikakis, Shevaun Hogan

Half-backs: Melissa Hickey, Kerryn Stephens, Yasmin Horsham

Centres: Natalie Wood, Daisy Pearce, Monique Kelly

Half-forwards: Anna McIlroy, Bronwyn Hutchinson, Lauren Arnell

Forwards: Jane Lange, Moana Hope, Kate Burke

Followers: Aasta O'Connor, Sarah Hammond, Kathy Zacharopoulos

Interchangers: Kris Gardiner, Anna Schwager, Georgina Thompson, Anna Brown

Coach: Peta Searle

Increasingly, though, I found that I just wasn't enjoying footy as much as I had before. I felt like I had achieved just about everything that was possible in the women's game. And I could not escape the feeling that people were continually judging me. Part of this was due to a lack of self-confidence. Being shy also didn't help. These traits turned me into a worried mess.

At the same time, my life was getting really hectic. I had moved out of Nicole Graves' house and into my own place in Glenroy. I was working full-time in traffic management. And I had decided to help out my family by providing food, clothing and somewhere to live to two of my nephews. I wanted and felt I needed to step up and help out in this way as my two older sisters had had nineteen children between them by this time, obviously following the big-family tradition. But they weren't coping, due to lack of support. Mum became concerned about the kids and took them all into her own home.

This is one of the best examples of why Mum is an inspiration to me. She should be made a saint before she dies. She is the most caring and generous person on the planet. Sometimes, in person or on social media, people say that I'm an inspiration to them, given my background and what I've managed to achieve. My answer is always the same: 'You haven't met my mum.' With nineteen kids living with her in her tiny place in Glenroy, I decided to muck in and help the family in the best way I could.

The Department of Human Services supported Mum by renovating her house to create extra rooms and a couple of bungalows out the back to accommodate everyone. Then somebody gave Mum a caravan that could be used as an extra room. I'm not really sure what the highest number of people living at Mum's place at one time was, but it would have been at least twenty-five. Crazy stuff. But I could tell that Mum's health was deteriorating due to the stress she was under. Really, helping out was the least I could do.

I had a good job and I had been able to afford to rent a decent place. But taking on my two nephews, who were only primary school age, markedly increased the level of stress in my life. I was only twenty-two, but I felt like I needed to support the two kids living with me as well as some of my brothers and sisters who were still living with Mum. It was a lot of pressure. But I have never been a person to take the easy way out. I have always been a person who wants to work hard and achieve things in life. As Mum said on the episode of *Australian Story* that featured us, 'Moana's always been wanting to work. I've never known Moana to be, you know, "I'll stay at home today" or, "I don't want to do this anymore".'

With so much on my plate, something had to give. I was feeling very insecure about myself, and those feelings were strongest when I was at the footy club. I started thinking about quitting, and then I started thinking about Dad. Then I started thinking about him passing away and how losing him still made me so sad. I suppose I had tried to suppress my sadness about Dad's passing for a long time. I had used sport as a way of avoiding the grief that I had suffered. I tried to think about nothing other than footy and cricket, and for a number of years this tactic had worked. But now that deep sadness started to grip me. I think I was finally starting to properly process Dad's death and what a loss it had been for me.

When those feelings combined with my suspicions that the people who were running women's footy hated me because of my short hair and tattoos, I spiralled into a real funk. For me this look had been the way I expressed myself, my way of me being me, so I couldn't understand why people would not accept that. My state of mind just got worse and I became depressed, which nobody knew about, because I never really told anyone.

I couldn't think of any other remedy apart from walking away from football. So I did it, but the decision sparked a new wave of negative emotions within me. I felt like I had let Dad down. He had encouraged me to chase my dreams, to be the best footballer that I could be, and now I had given up. And by walking away from the game, I felt I was losing my connection to him. But I was so angry at the way I had been treated and judged. I felt deeply scarred.

I played just one game for the Falcons early in the 2010 season, and then quit the club and stood out of the game for the rest of the year. I departed having played eighty-seven games and kicked 315 goals. I talked quite a bit with Nicole Graves during this time, and her thoughts on why my relationship with footy unravelled are interesting:

> She was always such a freaky, elite little player. But even in the middle of her time at Darebin, she went through some periods where she was thinking, 'Will I play footy, won't I play footy? I'm not really sure if I can be myself in this sport.' Mo is prone to going through those stages. What I now do for a living is nurture those kids, many of them Indigenous, who have that kind of crazy talent that no one really knows where it has come from. So I have spent time reflecting on how they compare to Mo. What I now know is if you don't support their flair and nurture their flair, then those players will say, 'Well, I can't do this anymore. I'm going to do something else.' That certainly happened to Mo at times when people didn't support her in the way she wanted, and I think that explains why she quit the game when she did.
>
> But, in defence of the people who were running the game back then, it was a very different time for women's footy. I don't blame those in charge of women's footy for doing what they did when they asked Mo to cover up her tattoos. I had been on the board of the Victorian Women's Football League for a time, so I knew what the people running the league were up against. The image of women's footy was that it was a bunch

of butch lesbians with short hair and tattoos playing a male-dominated sport. So they were trying to project an image to counter that stereotype. These days so many women have got tattoos and funky hairstyles that no one notices them. Those sorts of things are cool. Just look at how much people love Mo's tatts. It seems to me like the whole world is celebrating Mo's tattoos, which is really wonderful to see. But it was different back then.

The women's footy administrators were trying to grow the game and reassure parents that their little girls weren't going to be changed forever by playing some Aussie Rules. You look at how it is now, and every kid is encouraged to play, so it was just a different time. And Mo wasn't the only one who was told to cover up their tatts and look a bit more feminine for media appearances. There were several others who didn't quite fit the image and were asked to look a certain way. Some chose to conform and some told them to fuck off.

◆ ◆ ◆

Once I stopped playing footy, my life started to veer off the rails. This happened in two ways. First, I was so insecure about myself. I struggled to go out in public because I was worried that I was continually being judged. I had been so hurt by the league I started doubting all human interactions. I became scared of them and so I avoided them.

To try to combat my insecurity and shyness, I started drinking heavily. I was drunk basically every weekend. Once I was drunk and in party mode, I could be a totally different person. Even so, when I went out clubbing, which I did regularly, I was completely paranoid about going to the toilet. I would make a friend open the door of the toilets, and I would literally run in, do what I had to do, and then run out. I was so worried that people, thinking I was a boy, would call me a pervert or something for being in the women's toilets. The pressures of my life and all the things going on my head were pretty fraught and mixed up. On top of that, I had always been quite skinny and very fit, but now I was putting on weight and feeling like a slob. I was, to put it simply, pretty fucked up. It was a wasted year.

In early 2011, I decided I needed to try to get back into footy. I missed the camaraderie, and the feeling of being engrossed in a game, when getting your hands on the Sherrin is the only thing you think about. I joined the St Albans Spurs, but I only played two games before I lost interest again. The key problem was that I was still going out every Friday night, so I kept turning up to games hung over. Being in bad shape meant I couldn't do the things I wanted to on the field, which made me frustrated. The footy field had once been my safe haven. But now it was a place that made me unhappy. I had to confront the truth about the mess I was in. Instead I just wasted another year.

In 2012, I tried again to rekindle my love of football. I went back to the Spurs and played twelve games and kicked a very respectable forty-five goals. But I still couldn't escape the feeling that the people running women's footy wanted me to fail because I didn't fit their desire for the game to become a beauty pageant. Being in this terrible headspace even started to affect my work. I would get called into the office for a meeting and I would be paranoid about what I looked like, thinking, I'd better try to put my hair up in a ponytail or something, or they won't accept me. I couldn't shake that original rejection. It had derailed me.

Part II

Counterpoint

By 2013, I was lost. I was going out with my mates a lot and acting like a real party animal, but I wasn't happy. I wasn't physically happy. I wasn't mentally happy. I desperately wanted to fall in love with football again. It was the outlet from everyday life that I longed for and loved the most. Inside I felt football had the power to make me happy again.

I decided to go back to the Eastern Devils for the 2013 season. I played a few games early in the year but, like when I was at the St Albans Spurs, I really just went through the motions. I should have been working hard on the track to get myself back in shape, but instead I hardly went to training at all. There were a few times when I thought about giving up on footy for good.

I started mentioning these thoughts to one of my closest friends, Tegan, who I had been mates with since childhood. She told me that I wasting my talent. I should have cared about what she said, but I didn't. Then, one day, Tegan rang me and said, 'Hey, did you know there's going to be a footy match between the Western Bulldogs and Melbourne next week? And it's going to be played at the MCG.'

'What's so great about that?' I replied. 'The Bulldogs play Melbourne every year.'

'No, it's a women's game.'

You might find this hard to believe, given the game was being heavily promoted in the media at the time, but I didn't even know it was taking place. I was living in my own little world, which involved working hard, partying hard and being a foster mother to two young boys. As Tegan explained to me what the match was all about, I nearly dropped my phone.

'No way,' I said. 'There can't be a women's game between the Bulldogs and Melbourne. It's not possible.'

'Well, there is,' Tegan insisted. 'And we should go.'

As I later found out, the game was organised to form the centrepiece of the AFL's Women's Round, which had previously been mostly about paying tribute to the impact that women have on Aussie Rules footy off the field. But the AFL was now seriously thinking about creating a national women's competition sometime in the future, with each AFL club fielding a women's team. With this in mind, the Western Bulldogs and Melbourne had put their hands up to start the revolution by kitting out two teams made up of the best female footballers in Australia. What would be the first of six exhibition matches between the Dogs and Demons was subsequently held as a curtain-raiser to a men's match between the same sides.

I ummed and ahhed for a few days about going to the game. On a number of occasions I rang Tegan and said, 'Nah, I'm not going to go. I can't. It's probably going to be too confronting.'

To put it bluntly, I knew inside that if I had been fit and motivated I would have been one of the best female footballers in the nation. I could have been playing in that game. How could I just sit in the stands and watch these others run around and take all the glory?

A couple of days out from the game, Tegan wasn't giving up so easily. She rang again. She put on her most serious voice and said, 'Mo, this is bullshit. You have got to go.' So, on Sunday, 30 June 2013, we walked into the MCG and took our seats just as the teams were running out.

My former Darebin teammate Daisy Pearce led the Melbourne team onto the field. An Australia-wide draft had been held after the women's national championships to decide which players would represent the Demons and which players would represent the Dogs. Daisy had been chosen by Melbourne, which had the first pick in the draft. She looked so joyous as she jogged onto the MCG, and I was really happy for her.

As the players warmed up, I could hardly believe what I was seeing. It wasn't like when I last played in the national championships and we had just one coach and one trainer. These girls were being looked after by an army of coaches, fitness staff and water carriers. They were wearing AFL colours, and they were running around on the MCG. It was a complete head-spin.

'How did this happen?' I kept saying to Tegan. 'How did women's footy go from playing two games in a day in front of no one and getting drunk every night at my last national championships to these girls representing AFL clubs at the home of footy in brand-new gear?'

My jaw hit the floor once the game started. Even though it was a damp evening, the standard of footy was amazing. Daisy's

Melbourne team won by thirty-two points, which meant she received the Hampson–Hardeman Cup, a trophy that had been specially struck to honour Barb Hampson and Lisa Hardeman, who started the women's national championships back in the 1990s.

I walked out of the MCG that evening utterly inspired. As we were heading to the train, I gave Tegan a hug and exclaimed, 'That was fucking brilliant.'

I wanted to go to the gym right there and then, although I went to the pub instead, where I ran into Nicole Graves, who had come across from Western Australia to watch the game. We had a heap of drinks and a great time, and when we finally parted I said to Nicole, 'I'm going to play in the next one.'

6
Back in the game

THE FOLLOWING DAY I went and visited my mum. 'I'm going to devote myself to footy again,' I told her. She gave me a smile, then calmly stated, 'You make sure you do it your way.'

That comment really struck me. It was so meaningful, reminding me of the music we played at Dad's funeral. I nodded and repeated, 'I'm going back to footy and I'm definitely going to do it *my way*.'

Ten minutes later I was at my local gym signing a membership form. I was probably 15 or 20 kilograms overweight, but I was adamant that if I set my mind to it I could play in the next Western Bulldogs versus Melbourne game, which was set to take place the following year. I knew it was going to be a hard road; my body wasn't just going to bounce back into shape in a week. But, at the age of twenty-five, the resurrection of my football career had begun.

Even though I didn't play in that first exhibition match, I walked taller after it. My feeling was that women's footy was finally arriving on the big stage, and this was the theme of an article written by Samantha Lane in *The Age* following the game:

> The first AFL-sanctioned women's match has been declared a resounding success with the movement now set to receive unprecedented league support after winning a host of powerful new fans.
>
> A contest between Australia's most talented female footballers who played for Melbourne and the Western Bulldogs in a historic curtain-raiser to the corresponding men's fixture last Saturday at the MCG, will almost certainly be repeated in 2014 and may even happen twice next season. The grand plan is that a televised national women's competition will be functioning by 2020, and that some AFL clubs could adopt women's teams permanently.
>
> A crowd of about 3000 assembled for the start of the women's match and swelled to about 7500 by three-quarter-time—about 90 minutes before the start of the traditional main event that eventually drew 21,217 spectators.
>
> The three-quarter-time attendance for the female footy game—bigger than the crowds recorded for four Greater Western Sydney games this season—impressed AFL deputy chief executive Gillon McLachlan.
>
> 'I thought it was fantastic. I think that the talent in women's football is a story that we haven't told very well ... it's not something that we've pushed or told stories about,' McLachlan told Fairfax Media. 'I think this year is the first time we have, and I think it was certainly something that people wanted to know more about, and bought into.

> 'The fact that there were around 3000 people there for the start of the game, and around 7000 people there at three-quarter time, it's obvious that it has interest for a lot of people. I think that can be regarded as a great success.
>
> 'I think what is 100 per cent on the agenda now is that Australian rules football is a legitimate sporting option for all women ... we certainly think there is great scope to improve and evolve the stream of football for talented girls.'

I started going to the gym twice a day. I enrolled in a boxing program and I worked with the boxing coaches nearly every day. They were brutal sessions but they helped me rebuild my aerobic fitness and lose weight. My performances for the Eastern Devils improved out of sight.

I rang Emily Woods and told her about my epiphany. She was rapt:

> I mainly keep up to date these days with Mo on Facebook and Instagram and that sort of stuff, and I remember there was that period when she was hardly playing football and there were always pictures of her at clubs with drinks in her hands. I thought, 'Oh, it's such a waste of talent.' So I was really happy when she did devote herself to the game again. It was such a relief to see that her amazing talent wasn't going to waste.

All this made my life seriously hectic. I was now working in quite a senior role in traffic management, but I still had to get up at 3 or 4 am every day to plan where my crews were going to be.

Among the people in those crews were a number of my brothers and nephews, who I had hired so as to give them a chance to earn their own money and make a contribution to society. On top of that, I was trying to help Mum out as she battled various health problems.

In all this time, I never wavered from my commitment to get myself fit enough to play at the highest level, though. I continued to train really hard after the 2013 season ended, although those gym sessions were interrupted for a few weeks by a trip to the United States with Tegan and a few other mates, which I had planned long before I decided to return to footy. But while I was there I ran pretty much every day. I was so driven to be part of that next exhibition match.

Once I returned to Australia, I decided which team I was going to play club football with in 2014. I wanted a fresh start, so I didn't want to go back to the Devils or the Falcons. A few of my good friends were playing for the St Kilda Sharks, a club based at the aptly named Peanut Farm Reserve, not far from St Kilda Beach. I liked the idea of playing for the Sharks, but I wanted to make sure I would be going to a club that was really going to believe in me and develop me as a person and as a footballer. There was another catch as well. Mum's health had been deteriorating further, so I had agreed to become the main carer for my severely disabled sister, Livinia. I needed to know that the Sharks would not only take me for who I was, but be just as welcoming to Livinia, who would often need to come with me to the club.

I knew the Sharks were the ones for me after I met with their coach at the time, Shannon McFerrin, who's a legend in women's football. Shannon completely understood where I was coming from.

'Come over to us,' she said. 'We'll take care of you, and Livinia is welcome at the club any time.' She was true to her word. Everyone at the Sharks played a role in getting me back on my feet over the next few years, and the people at the club treat Livinia as if she were their own child.

Interestingly enough, one of the people heavily involved with the Sharks when I signed up was Leesa Catto, who had relinquished her role as media manager for the VWFL some years earlier. Early on in my time with the Sharks, we had an important talk and I explained to her the way I felt after she asked me to cover my tattoos for the photo shoot in 2009. Leesa was quite taken aback by my version of events. She did not know that I had been so hurt by what she said. To her great credit, she was very apologetic and we have been on good terms ever since. She later explained from her point of view what happened:

> I didn't really know Mo at the time, but I knew that she was a very good player, as were the other women who I teed up for the photo. I didn't want any of them to have visible tattoos. It was nothing about Mo. It was never anything personal about her. I had no idea about the meaning of her tattoos at the time, that they related to her family and her father in particular. I didn't want visible tattoos in the photo.
>
> Mo and I discussed the whole thing before we appeared on *Australian Story*. I apologised to her, because I never considered the impact that it may have had on her at the time, and I had never thought about it in the years since. I just didn't think it was an issue. But I can see now that it contributed to her finding herself in a not-so-good place.

When I started out at the Sharks, I felt at home straightaway. There was a great feeling around the club, and you'd go to training and everyone was laughing and having fun and telling jokes. It was exactly the kind of atmosphere that I needed. During the early part of the 2014 season I worked my way into some pretty decent form. I was back at full-forward, back kicking goals, and having the time of my life. The season would continue to get better and better for me, and I ended up kicking eighty-seven goals, including seventeen one afternoon against Bendigo. I also won the Sharks' best and fairest.

About a quarter of the way through that season I decided it was worth nominating for the second women's draft, which was held to decide the make-up of the teams for the second exhibition match between Melbourne and the Western Bulldogs. But this time it was a draft to top up the squads from the year before. I really wasn't sure if I had done enough to be picked, so I was absolutely rapt when the Dogs chose me with pick ten. All of that hard work in the gym had paid off. My dream of playing for an AFL club was on the verge of coming true. Now I just had to do enough in the ensuing training sessions to make sure I got a game.

On the day of my first training session with the Dogs, I was gripped by anxiety. As I drove into the car park at the Whitten Oval in Footscray, I could hardly breathe. I was soon suffering from a full-scale panic attack. I started thinking, I'm going to walk in there, they're going to see my tatts, and they'll judge me straightaway. They won't accept me. I had a long-sleeved t-shirt on, but I was so worried about what the other players and staff would think when I had to get changed into my footy gear. I sat there for a minute or two. Nope. I can't do it. I rang Tegan.

'I can't go in there,' I said. 'They're going to look at me and tell me to go home.' I was crying. Tegan did her best to reassure me.

'I promise you that won't happen,' she said. 'You have to go in there. It will be the greatest regret of your life if you don't. And you don't want to be a person who is filled with regrets.' She was right. I had to dig deep into my reserves of strength and go in there. 'Okay,' I replied. 'I'm going to do it.' I didn't want to let her down. She was trying so hard to keep me on track.

Before getting out of my car, I reached into my bag and pulled out a packet of Xanax, a powerful anti-anxiety drug that I had been prescribed by my local doctor. I swallowed two of the tablets, took a deep breath, then grabbed my bag and walked into the change rooms. Even after taking the tablets, I was still on edge. I tried not to make eye contact with anyone. Then I spied a bag of Bulldogs stuff with my name on it. I sat down and looked in the bag. There were so many items of clothing in there, including a brand-new footy jumper. It was all for me, and it was free.

Looking at all the gear made me seriously happy. But my mood kept swinging wildly. When it was time to get changed I suddenly felt sick. People were going to look at me when I took my top off. Someone was sure to say, 'We don't want people with tattoos all over them on our team.' Eventually I ripped off my t-shirt and pulled on a long-sleeved Bulldogs jumper. No one said anything. I sighed with relief.

Once I was out on the training track I was fine. Peta Searle, my old coach from the Falcons—there were now nine ex-Falcons players in the Bulldogs' squad—was in charge, and she helped me settle down. I soon became completely engrossed in the training session. Everyone on the track was a really good player and the skills on show were amazing. Every time I led for the ball, it would be delivered lace-out in front of my eyes. There seemed to be some really good spirit in the team, with everyone dishing out plenty of high-fives and pats on the back. Having been filled with nerves when I arrived at the club, I was now having a huge amount of fun. I remember thinking, Whoa, this game is so great. I love it.

A few days later, the teams for the game were announced. I was named as full-forward for the Bulldogs. I was so stoked, and everyone in my family was super happy as well. But then came another seriously nerve-wracking time. The plan was for our team to meet at an inner-city hotel in Melbourne two days before the game. The idea was that we could hang out together and get to know each other, and do some light training (we hadn't yet trained with some members of our squad because they were based interstate), in that time before the match.

I felt sick in the hours before heading to the hotel. I was on the verge of vomiting all the time. I was so gripped by anxiety about what might go down while we were there. So many of the other girls in the team were the clean-cut and ponytail-wearing types that the footy administrators love. I was sure that they would weigh me up and think I was doing damage to their cause with my tattoos and short hair. I was so scared that I would meet one of the Bulldogs officials and they would say to me, 'Who the fuck are you? The person running water?'

My greatest fear was any team-bonding exercise, where we took turns to speak about ourselves to the rest of the group. I was sure I would say something dumb and everyone would laugh at me. I was in such a state and I was having conversations with Peta Searle in my head, saying, 'Please don't, please don't do a team exercise. I don't want to talk, I don't want to talk.' I was always worried that everyone else was so much better educated than me. So I was like, 'Man, I don't want to answer any questions. What if I say the wrong word?' I was also freaked out by the prospect of any team exercise that involved writing on a whiteboard. What if they make me write on that board? I can't write. I can't spell. If they ask me to write a word and I spell it wrong, people will laugh at me.

I took a couple of Xanax before heading to the hotel. But as I walked towards the check-in desk, I almost had another panic attack. I remembered that we had to share rooms. This really worried me. I was certain that my roommate would think I was a dumb bogan. You cannot believe how relieved I was when I found out that my roommate was Emma Carney. I had played cricket with Emma and had always felt that she was a kind and caring person. I had never felt like she was judging me. In fact, she is one of the loveliest people I have met in my sporting career.

Nevertheless, when I got up to our room I just wanted to stay there. I was that nervous about interacting with all the other players. When I finally emerged for dinner, I sat next to Emma but hardly said a word. I remember some of the other girls saying, 'Mo, you're the quietest person I've ever met.' I just didn't want to talk to anybody by this stage because I was so certain that they were all examining my every move. But with Emma's support, I slowly came out of my shell. I talked to Emma a lot and that helped me get the confidence I needed to get involved in conversations with the others. After that I always tried to sit next to Emma in team meetings, because she was like a security blanket for me.

Even though the sick feeling in the pit of my stomach started to go away that night, the only time I felt completely at ease during those two days was when we had a training session at Etihad Stadium. When I am chasing a footy, my mind becomes so focussed. Nothing else worries me. And the buzz from being allowed to train on an AFL venue was electric. For so long, female footballers had been second-class citizens in our own sport. Finally, we were being treated with the respect we deserved.

The thing that would make my anxiety disappear completely was pulling on my Bulldogs jumper prior to the game. For me, it was like putting on a superhero costume. As soon as I had that jumper on I felt like I could take on the world. When we ran through our banner and out onto the ground I looked around the stadium and thought, Wow, this is pretty extraordinary. I could hear numerous members of my family cheering me on from the stands. What a journey I had been on. Twelve months before, I had been an overweight mess. Now I was playing for an AFL club at an AFL venue. It was unreal.

I felt in the zone right throughout the match. Although we lost by forty-six points, I was able to get the better of my opponent and kick three of our four goals. I kicked the first goal of the game, which was a long set shot from out near the boundary. My other two goals were snaps, and they got a great response from the crowd. As I high-fived my teammates after kicking my second snap goal, I could hear the crowd really roaring. My inner voice was like, They seem to think I'm okay. They are accepting me. It was a tremendous feeling.

When we returned to our change rooms after the game, I didn't want to take my footy jumper off. This time it was nothing to do with people seeing my tatts and looking down on me. It was that I wanted to keep feeling like I had a superhero costume on. I feel deflated whenever I take off my footy jumper after a match. I'm like, I'll just have to go back to being me again. That's exactly how

I felt on this occasion. Wearing that Dogs jumper and playing at Etihad Stadium had made me feel a million dollars. During the game, after I kicked those snap goals, I felt like people were staring at me for a good reason. But I knew that when I took my jumper off it would feel like I was crashing back to reality. And that's exactly how it panned out. I took my jumper off and my mind went, Oh fuck, I'm a normal person again.

Anxiety is such a hard thing to shake. Even though I had played so well for the Western Bulldogs in 2014, and later that season had won the Sharks' best and fairest and been the club's leading goal kicker, I still had a lot of self-esteem issues bubbling away inside me. Sometimes I went to functions and whether they were something to do with the AFL exhibition games or the VWFL, I would wear a headband over my hair and make sure I had my arms covered. Sometimes I found myself thinking, Maybe if I just grow my hair everything will be okay. I couldn't wear dresses to functions, because I have never felt comfortable in a dress, but I went through a phase of wearing really tight jeans and girly high-heeled shoes. But this just made me feel like an idiot, and I wasn't being true to myself. I was trying to change to meet the expectations of others, which is never a good thing.

My mental state was still all over the place prior to the third Western Bulldogs versus Melbourne exhibition in 2015. When I arrived at the Whitten Oval for my first training session with the Victorian members of the Bulldogs' squad, I was again gripped by fear. I suddenly didn't want to get out of the car and I didn't want to walk into the change rooms. In the back of my mind a little monster was telling me that something bad was going to happen. Someone was finally going to decide that I didn't fit the look that the AFL wanted for women's footy. It was like I was in a dream and I thought that any minute now I would wake up and my career in the AFL would be gone.

It took another call to Tegan and some more Xanax to calm me down. As happended the year before, I was fine out on the training track, but when I was just hanging around with the other girls I felt so self-conscious. I felt like they were being critical of me all the time, even though I'm sure that most of them weren't. Once again, Emma Carney helped me out a great deal. When I turned up at our team hotel, I found out that I was rooming with someone other than Emma and I nearly started crying on the spot. Thankfully, our team manager changed things around and I was able to be in the same room as Emma. That was a massive relief.

As it turned out, there was a much bigger issue in the lead-up to that exhibition game, which was played at the MCG on a Sunday morning in May, prior to an AFL match between the Bulldogs and Melbourne. On the Saturday night I received a call from Mum telling that my older brother Corey was in intensive care. I think he had contracted pneumonia, then picked up another bug that made him swell up like a puffer fish. As I sat in my hotel room with Emma, Mum told me that Corey had died in his hospital bed before being brought back to life. Mum was very emotional. She said the doctors didn't know if he was going to make it. I have to pull out of the team, I thought. I have to be there for my brother. Family comes first.

It turned out that Corey had been taken to hospital that morning, but Mum hadn't told me because she didn't want to interrupt my preparations for the game. Even now, as she talked to me with such emotion in her voice, she told me that all the family wanted me to play. They wanted me to experience running around on the MCG. They needed something to be proud of at such a tough time. So I bottled up my feelings and went back to thinking about the game.

I carried a lot of emotional baggage onto the MCG that morning. But I was still able to soak up the experience of playing at the home of footy. It was mind blowing to be out there representing an AFL club. There weren't many people in the stands when our game began, but I didn't care. Just to be out on that ground with the best female footballers in the nation was good enough. One of the great things about this particular game was that it was telecast by Channel Seven, so many of my family members were able to watch it while they were visiting Corey in hospital.

I struggled to get into the game in the first half, as did many of my teammates. To be fair, Melbourne probably should have had the game in the bag by half time, yet their poor kicking—3.8 (26) to 2.3 (15) at the long break—kept us in it. Midway through the third quarter, with us trailing by twelve points, I marked a great pass from Stephanie Chiocci in the right forward pocket. I was on a really tough angle, so I decided to go for a banana kick, and it went right through the middle. Early in the last quarter, another great chance came my way when Jessica Wuetschner, who had come across from Western Australia to play in the match, kicked a ball in my direction in the left pocket. The ball bounced in front of me, but I managed to grab it cleanly, evade my opponent, then shrug off two tackles and snap a goal. I punched the air with delight. Suddenly, the margin was just two points. A few minutes later I had a shot to give us the lead. I desperately wanted it to go through, not only for my team but also for my family watching at the hospital. To my immense disappointment, the kick went wide. Melbourne then raced the ball up the other end and scored a late goal, which made the final margin eight points.

It was a disappointing way to finish a great experience, but over the coming weeks my family was able to enjoy a victory of sorts. I don't know how he did it, but Corey miraculously pulled through. His fight against the illness was so much bigger than anything I've been through in my life, and I think it helped to put all my battles into perspective.

7
Susan's way

THROUGH PLAYING IN the exhibition games I was able to meet all kinds of interesting people. However, none of them have had a greater impact on my life than Susan Alberti. I met her for the first time when she addressed the Western Bulldogs' women's squad in the lead-up to the exhibition match against Melbourne in 2014. I will never forget the moment I first laid eyes on her at the Whitten Oval. We had just finished training and were sitting around on plastic chairs having something to eat. A number of the girls had been told that Sue was coming to see us, and they were really excited. They thought of her as the 'Queen of Women's Footy'.

I don't know what I was expecting, but I was so shocked when she walked into the room. She had this extraordinary hairdo and was carrying a Dolce & Gabbana handbag and wearing a pearl necklace. The pearls really struck me. The only time I had seen pearls before was in the movie *Titanic*, when the posh people on board that ship were wearing them. I had no idea who she was. I was thinking, Who is this lady, and why is she here? I didn't know she was the club's vice-president.

As she started walking around the room and chatting to the girls, I began feeling extremely anxious. I thought, Fuck, she's going to look at me. She's going to stare at me for too long. She's going to judge me. A person like her is going to think I'm some kind of animal, with my tatts and no ponytail. I was heading straight into full panic attack mode, so I tried to avoid eye contact with her. I really didn't want to have to talk to her. With, She's really going to think I'm a loser if she hears me speak, being the main thought coursing through my brain, I was silently begging, Please don't ask me a question.

The funny thing is that some judgemental thoughts did pop into Susan's head when she met me, as she said much later on *Australian Story*: 'When I first met her I kept thinking, "How could a beautiful young woman (and she is beautiful, she really is beautiful) want to cover herself in tattoos?" So I did judge her, but I was so wrong and I will admit that.'

Despite all of this, it wasn't long until I started warming to Sue. She had come to see us and tell us her life story and about a cause close to her heart, the Susan Alberti Medical Research Foundation. She started by telling us how she grew up in a housing commission home and that her family could rarely afford nice things. I could relate. Wow, I kept thinking, what an amazing journey she must have been on. It was clear that her wealth and status had not been presented to her on a silver platter.

Sue also told us about how she and her first husband, Angelo Alberti, built up a hugely successful property development business,

Dansu Constructions. Then she shared with us the heartbreak of losing Angelo, who died in 1995 after being knocked off his bike by a truck. The most powerful part of Sue's talk, though, was about her daughter, Danielle, who was a very talented artist and was diagnosed with Type 1 diabetes at a young age. She told us how Danielle went to live in New York despite her illness, and how she, Sue, had been very worried about her deteriorating health. I struggled to contain my own emotions when Sue told us about how her daughter was eventually approved for a kidney transplant, which was to take place in Australia. She said she travelled to New York so that she could fly home with Danielle, but the end of that story is heart-breaking.

Later she would talk about the flight home on *Australian Story*:

> And about an hour out of Los Angeles, Danielle started thrashing around and wanting to take off her clothes, and I thought, 'This is really odd.' She said, 'Mum, my back is so painful.' I said, 'Don't worry, I'll rub it.' She said, 'Will you hold me, Mum?' And I did, and I sat there on the side of her seat holding her, and with that she had a massive heart attack and she died in my arms. I laid next to her for the next nine hours or ten hours bringing her home to Australia, not alive but dead.

Thinking about Sue being in that terrible situation still sends a shiver down my spine. But on the day she visited us she wasn't telling us these stories to gain our sympathy. She wanted us to know that no matter how tough life can be at times, resilience and strength can lead to better days. That was a message I really appreciated and related to. While she has a chauffeur who drives her around in an expensive Mercedes, right then I felt like I genuinely had some things in common with her.

The next time I saw Sue was in our change rooms after the game. Even though her story had inspired me, I still felt intimidated by her. But when I saw her standing by herself at one stage, I found some courage and thought, What the heck. I'm going to stir her up a bit. The people at the St Kilda Sharks, a club she has given a lot of financial support to over the years, often referred to her as 'The Queen' or 'Her Majesty'. I remember that I went over to her and made some wisecrack about that and about how it would take a hurricane to move her hair. I was thinking, She's either going to get my humour or she's not. Fortunately, Sue laughed at my banter, I breathed a sigh of relief, and since then an amazing friendship has developed between us.

I have learned so much more about her story in the past couple of years. I have learned about her battle with cancer, her open-heart surgery and how she went through a stage of putting on weight before she was given a stern talking to by a doctor, then used her steely resolve to lose 48 kilograms and keep it off. On top of all that, she is one of the most generous people on the planet. She has given away more money than I can imagine ever earning. The amount she has donated to various causes is said to be more than $25 million, not that she has ever shared those kinds of numbers with me. According to a number of feature stories written about her, she has donated $15 million to medical research, including to scientists who are trying to develop both a vaccine and a cure for Type 1 diabetes, a cause that is painfully close to her heart.

Sue is truly an extraordinary woman. And that's before you take into account her fight against sexism, which saw her sue Sam

Newman after he denigrated her on *The Footy Show* a few years ago. Sue's effort to win that case, (she then donated the $220,000 settlement to charity) struck a great blow for women's rights.

Sue and I have been able to bond by speaking honestly about the fact we had both judged each other on our first meeting, even though our life stories have some similarities. It was so shit of me to have judged her based purely on what she looked like, when I hated people doing that to me. I remember looking at her and thinking, Oh, you've got pearls and a driver and millions of dollars, you must be a typical rich and snobby person. Of course, my first reaction should have been, I wonder what she is like as a person? That's how I want people to approach me. It was a breakthrough for me to reflect on this.

As I said earlier, Sue also regretted thinking about me this way. But once we started hanging out a bit, we were both like, Wow, you are amazing. As she said on *Australian Story*:

> I got to know more and more about her background and I found out what a very solid, wonderful person she was. Not only a good footballer, she'd done it so tough. She'd had the hard school of knocks like myself and immediately we had a rapport, the two of us.

We realised that we are both good people on the inside, even if we look completely different on the outside. And this realisation did so much to reduce my levels of anxiety generally about the issue of how people might view me. It was, without wanting to overstate it, a massive turning point in my life. It means so much to me that a person as accomplished and successful as Sue is happy to take me for who I am. These days, Sue often invites me to functions to support the Susan Alberti Medial Research Foundation, and she often speaks super highly of me in her speeches. When she does, I just think, Wow, the people at these functions are the cream of society and here she is telling them about me and how good I am. The fact that she is proud of me has made me proud of myself.

Thinking back to the first few times that I spoke to Sue, the thing that actually blew me away the most was her revelation that she had been a serious football player in her younger days. I could not believe that a person who was so prim and proper could once have been out there in the mud chasing a footy around. But that was the truth of the matter. She and her brother, Richard Jenkings, talked about her younger days on *Australian Story*:

> Richard: Sue is almost a dichotomy in her personality. When she was a child she was mischievous, daring, lovable, at times very, very girlie. At other times when she felt like it, which was in the backyard with me, she'd tough it out with me playing football.
>
> Susan: I really wanted to play serious football. I was a pretty tough rover, I was a tough tackler and Dad used to think I was pretty good. But then, by about the age of fifteen, Dad didn't think it was safe for a young woman, particularly as I was playing against, well, mature men, so I had to hang up my boots at fifteen.
>
> Richard: That was in the fifties, late fifties, she had no opportunity really to partake in a team. There were no girls' teams.

> Susan: When I couldn't continue playing football, I was absolutely heartbroken because the love of the game has been there since I was about six years old and it still continues to this day.

Finding out that she had been a footballer in her younger days was a huge revelation. I now understood why she was so passionate about footy and why she had devoted herself to the game to the point where she had become the first female vice-president of the Western Bulldogs. I now also realised why a few years earlier she had written a cheque for $25,000 to the VWFL, which basically saved the competition from going bankrupt—and this was on top of the thousands and thousands of dollars that she has donated to the Bulldogs over the years. And I understood why I often saw her standing at the back of the huddle at St Kilda Sharks games, with a twinkle in her eye that suggested she wished she could take off her expensive clothes, put on some footy gear, and run around with us.

Finding out that Sue had played footy made me feel so much better about myself. If a respected person like her had played women's footy and was prepared to back the game with her own money, then all of us who played the game clearly had some serious firepower in our camp. We weren't just a bunch of butch lesbians, as so many people seemed to think. We were a group of athletes from many different backgrounds and with many different ways of being in the world who deserved to be respected.

My relationship with Sue became stronger when we both appeared in that episode of *Australian Story* in 2016. Funnily enough, women's footy wasn't even in the original plans for the episode, as Sue recalls:

> *Australian Story* was initially going to be about my support and passion for medical research, but I told them there's a bigger thing out there that I'm really involved in. I told them that I really wanted to promote women's football and asked them what they thought about that. The producers thought it was a great idea, so I nominated Mo to be part of the story and that's how we became close. We really got to know one another and we really bonded during the four months that the cameras followed us around. It went on and on and on and on! We were together so much and we had so much of our lives to share. Of course, we look so different. When we met for lunch at a cafe in Toorak, she was there in her tracksuit pants and t-shirt and I was wearing one of my tailored suits. But we have a lot in common. We are from similar backgrounds, the school of hard knocks. We both grew up in public housing. And I like to help young women, particularly if they've got aspirations and they're talented, too. And she is.

Sue and I spent a lot of time together during the filming and joked around a lot with each other. We just clicked. I felt like I was hanging out with an older version of me. Sue loves joking around, and she is funny. She'll also tell you how it is when she feels the need. She's no fake. I think that's the key to her.

The highlight of our time together for *Australian Story* came when Sue visited my mum's house. The funniest part was when one of the show's producers said to me, 'How would you feel if Sue came to Glenroy? Her driver will take her over there in her Mercedes.' I was like, 'A Mercedes driving down my mum's street? That has never happened. And if it has happened before, it must have been stolen or the driver must have been frickin' lost.' I then joked to the producer, 'I'm happy to park it for her when she gets there, but it might not be there when she comes back out!'

The producer also asked me if my mum, whose health was deteriorating, would be stressed about someone like Susan Alberti visiting her home. But I quickly put him at ease. My mum is one of the most easygoing people on the planet. Even if the Queen were coming over, Mum wouldn't suddenly want to change her house. She wouldn't go around trying to fix everything up. She'd just say to the Queen, 'Here you go, have a seat on my chair that I bought from the op shop. Here's a cup of tea with normal tea bags and normal milk, and, sorry, but we don't have biscuits around here. By the way, how's your day going?' That would be my mum. So I knew that Mum wouldn't be freaked out by Susan coming to her place. She was never going to react like, 'Oh, you're this rich lady, so I had better try and act like someone I'm not.' She's as authentic as Sue is. And that's exactly how it all panned out.

Mum didn't do anything out of the ordinary before Sue arrived. She didn't do a big spring clean; she didn't set things up trying to be posh. She was actually in the middle of setting up a birthday party for a family member, so there was stuff everywhere. The house was messy as hell, but she didn't care. Because Mum is one of those people who says, 'You either accept me or you don't. And this is my house, so this is how it is.'

Still, it was funny when the big moment came and Sue's Mercedes pulled up out the front. She got out, looking like the Queen, and walked into the humble old housing commission home where I had grown up. Yet this is the thing about Sue: she might look all high and mighty, but she's so down to earth, so she and Mum got along like a house on fire. We all sat around and had a cup of tea and then Susan wandered back out to her Mercedes—thankfully, it was still there!—and headed off.

Sue says of her visit:

> You know what, it reminded me so much of my own old home. There was so much coming and going of people. I had never seen anything like that in my life. It was clearly a halfway house, with a bungalow here, a shed there and a caravan out the back. But it was spotlessly clean. That's the thing I noticed the most. You see, my mum kept our house like that. She was very proud of what she had, as is Mo's mother, Rosemary. And everyone was so friendly and warm when I visited. I think they probably thought that, given I turned up in a chauffeur-driven car, I was going to be a bit of a snob. Well, I wasn't. I was anything but. They were warm, I was warm, and we all got on really well. Rosemary is just gorgeous. I asked her if she knew the names of all the people living in the house at the moment. She just looked at me with a smile and said, 'No way. I haven't got time for that.' We all had a laugh. It was a really lovely occasion.

I have been to Sue's workplace and, as I mentioned, to lots of functions with her, including the 2016 Brownlow Medal Count, but I still haven't been to her fancy house. I assume it's like the place where the Queen lives. I remember watching the full version of the *Australian Story* episode and seeing her standing in front of plates that were on display there. No doubt they were worth a trillion dollars. I thought, Why would you have plates on display?

But then I came to a conclusion: The Queen would have plates on display, so that must be why.

Last year, not long before we appeared at a charity breakfast to promote women's footy, Sue gave me a string of pearls. I then wore them to the breakfast. When Sue was speaking, she referred to the fact that I was wearing pearls. I then yelled out, 'I promise I didn't steal them!' Everyone laughed, including Sue. That's the kind of mates we are. Classic Aussie mates who love and respect each other but are only too keen to take the piss out of each other and ourselves when we get the chance.

8

Collingwood calling

THE WOMEN'S EXHIBITION matches that were played between the Western Bulldogs and Melbourne in 2013, 2014 and 2015 were so successful that the AFL found itself under pressure to bring forward the planned start date for its national women's competition. Of course, it wasn't just those exhibition games that created the momentum for the AFL to get its act together sooner. The AFL's own participation statistics showed that women's footy was booming, with almost 400,000 females around the nation playing the game, which was a 20 per cent increase on the year before.

This led to the announcement in February 2016 that the AFL would indeed launch its women's league earlier than it had initially planned. It had been due to commence in 2020, but was now going to begin in 2017—just twelve months away—and this created much excitement among the women's football community. It was quite amazing to hear AFL chief executive Gillon McLachlan outline that he wanted to launch an eight-team competition, with games to be played in most capital cities during the following February and March. 'There's a revolution going on,' he said during a press conference that was held after the announcement. 'I've stuck my neck out with the 2017 as opposed to a bit later. There's been concern around the depth. But the success of the academies, the talent searches … means that I think next year … it looks more like eight teams rather than six.'

I couldn't quite believe it. In the space of just three years, female footballers had gone from being laughed at to being elevated onto the national stage. I felt a lot of pride at having played my part in building up women's footy.

To prepare for the new competition, a whole series of women's exhibition games was planned, featuring matches in a number of states. There were derbies between West Coast and Fremantle, Sydney and Greater Western Sydney and the Brisbane Lions and Gold Coast. There were also state games between teams representing South Australia, New South Wales/Australian Capital Territory, Tasmania and the Northern Territory. In addition to all that, two games were scheduled between the Western Bulldogs and Melbourne. The first was set down for March, with the second to be played as a stand-alone feature match on the weekend before the AFL finals, on which the AFL had decided to schedule a general bye so that all the teams playing in the finals could have a rest before starting the battle for the premiership.

It soon emerged that each team granted a licence to compete in the inaugural AFL Women's competition—only eight of the AFL's eighteen clubs were to be awarded licences for the first season—would be given the opportunity to sign 'marquee' players prior to

Appetite for life. Me and Dad at home in Glenroy in 1989.

The station wagon that ferried us around. Of course not all of us had a designated seat …

My family posse on a road trip to Brisbane. Always enough members for a kick-to-kick.

Perfecting the grip. The Sherrin looks so much bigger when you're small.

True colours. I loved the Hadfield Football Club, because their jumpers matched my beloved team, Hawthorn. I am the in the second row, at the far right in the Under 10s team photo from 1996.

My mum, who is my inspiration.

Listening to the coach at half-time. On the ground with Emily Woods and my sister Bree in Hadfield's open-age women's team.

The Australian International Rules football team that travelled to Ireland in 2006. I'm kneeling third from left.

All in the family. Practising my ball skills before my Darebin Falcons Grand Final in 2006 with nine of my siblings looking on. *Sebastian Costanzo/Fairfax Syndication*

Mutual admiration society. Susan Alberti and me post-match.

Left: Kicking the ton. A record 100 goals in the women's 2016 VFL season playing for the St Kilda Sharks. *Tim Carrafa/Newspix*

Larking around. The marquee players for the inaugural 2017 women's AFL competition. *Wayne Ludbey/Newspix*

Dabbing. Teaching Gillon McLachlan the finer points of dabbing at the announcement of the 2017 AFLW marquee players in July 2016. *Collingwood Football Club*

Hero worship. Vinny and I are rapt to meet Eddie McGuire, president of the Collingwood Football Club. *Collingwood Football Club*

My date, with her trademark pearls, at the Brownlow Medal Count in September 2016. *Pat Scala/Fairfax Media*

A dream come true. Training with Lauren Tesoriero at Collingwood in January 2017. *Robert Keeley Images*

Premier AFLW's match against Carlton at Ikon Park on 3 February in front of 24, 000 spectators. The atmosphere was electric. *Michael Willson/ AFL Media*

My first goal for the 2017 AFLW season against Melbourne. Finally!
Michael Dodge/AFL Media

One of the few photos I have of the family together at a nephew's baptism in 2016.

the national draft that would distribute the rest of the talent among the new teams. The marquee players were to receive the highest payments. So that meant everyone wanted to be a marquee player, and everyone wanted to play well in the exhibition matches that were to take place throughout the 2016 season.

I certainly had the ambition to be a marquee player in the back of my mind when I lined up for the Western Bulldogs against Melbourne at Highgate Reserve in Craigieburn on 2 March 2016. I went into the game super fit, after doing a summer program run by a new business called Acceleration, and I did my reputation no harm by giving my opponent the runaround and being named third-best player. 'Bulldogs forward Hope proved a massive problem for the Demons defence with her marking prowess and strength to hold a position in the contest,' was how the AFL website's match report saw my efforts. 'Hope booted three goals from strong marks in quick succession late in the first quarter to open up what would be a decisive break.' Those words 'decisive break' explain the best thing that came out of the day. At long last, we beat the Demons. The final scores were 6.5 (41) to 3.3 (21), and afterwards we sang our version of the Bulldogs song ('Girls of the West' rather than 'Sons of the West') with some serious gusto. It was a great relief to get that first victory on the board, and we had a good party to celebrate.

After that I headed back to the St Kilda Sharks for the start of the VWFL season. I was full of confidence following my performance for the Bulldogs. My previous two seasons with the Sharks, in which I had kicked eighty-seven goals in 2014 and another sixty-eight in 2015, also gave me great belief in myself.

I started the season in style. I kicked four goals in our round one win over the Eastern Devils, then I booted ten against

Bendigo the following week. But my thoughts were dominated by what was happening with the AFL competition. In early July came another big announcement, when the eight clubs that had been awarded licences were revealed. They were Collingwood, Carlton, the Western Bulldogs, Melbourne, Adelaide, the Brisbane Lions, Greater Western Sydney and Fremantle. 'Our game is on the cusp of changing forever, and for the better,' AFL commission chairman Mike Fitzpatrick said at the announcement at the MCG. 'The concept of a national competition has been put together in a short space of time, but this day has been a long time coming. The number of women and girls playing club football has doubled over the past five years. Female participation [has reached] 25 per cent of the total number of Australians playing our Indigenous game.'

It was all so exciting, but for those of us who knew we were in the best twenty or thirty players in Australia, it was a nerve-wracking time as well. I couldn't stop thinking, Could I be a marquee player? Will the Bulldogs want me? What if a big club like Collingwood or Carlton wants to talk to me? It was all so surreal.

I just assumed that all the clubs, particularly those based in Victoria, would apply for licences to field teams in the women's competition. So I remember being gutted when I read that Hawthorn was not even going to put in a bid for a licence. The Hawks released a statement with these comments from their chief executive, Stuart Fox: 'The prospect of a Hawthorn women's team in the future is an exciting one. However, at this time we believe that our most sustainable contribution will be made by investing in women's football at a grassroots level. We have some core programs and relationships in place that we can leverage to deliver ongoing investment into women's football.'

I had still very much considered myself a Hawthorn supporter, but I totally gave up on them after that happened. I thought to myself, I grew up barracking for you, I bought your jumpers, I went to your games. I fought for you against my family, who were all Essendon, and for no good reason you don't want to be involved in women's footy. Like, who do you think you are? There are a lot of women and girls who follow you, and you're trying to tell me you don't want them to fulfil their dreams? Or even those men who follow you, they've got daughters, what about their dreams? And you didn't even come out with a decent explanation. There was no way that I could continue to support a club that didn't support women's footy.

In a later meeting with Hawthorn, I was relieved to discover that Hawthorn's approach was to field a VFL team before applying for an AFLW licence to ensure they were appropriately set up. Geelong applied to be part of the AFL Women's league, then opted to field a team in the VFL because they missed out on getting an AFL licence.

Most of the Melbourne-based clubs who were granted licences to play in the inaugural AFL Women's league got in touch with me. Richmond and St Kilda had also contacted me, but they both missed out on getting licences. The clubs I spoke to seemed like they were mainly trying to gauge how keen I was to play at the highest level. I told them that I was dead keen to get a chance to prove myself.

Below the surface, however, I felt deeply insecure for the same old reasons. I worried that all the progress I had made was somehow going to come to nothing. By now I had my own manager, James Pitcher from Precision Sports Entertainment Group, who had approached me about joining his team, and he was starting to come to grips with my wavering self-confidence. When I had first signed with his management group, I had said to him, 'Mate, I need to be upfront with you. The AFL are not going to use me for anything.'

He asked, 'Why?'

'Because of how I look. They will want the girls who are the most feminine looking, and that's it. So don't be upset when I don't get any gigs, because I've dealt with it and I've moved on. I just want to play footy.'

James was a bit taken aback by my attitude.

'You've got to be kidding,' he said. 'You're the most marketable player in the game right now because you're different. That's how we see it.'

'Mate, it's not going to happen. People won't want a bar of me.'

'Wait and see,' he told me.

A while later, James and I were chatting and he asked if I was still keen on being a marquee player. His question was well timed, because I was starting to have doubts. I said to him, 'Can I just be a contracted player and not a marquee?' I asked about this because I was starting to feel very anxious about the types of appearances that I would have to do if I were a marquee player, and to worry that the club I was recruited by would want me to change the way I looked. I was certain that no club would want a marquee player with tattoos and short hair. And I had heard that each club would have two marquee players and five contracted players, so my hope was I could join a club as a contracted player and then fly under the radar.

'Marquee players have to do appearances, and people are not going to like me to go to things because I have tattoos, and it's going to make me feel shit about myself and I won't play good football because I'm going to be depressed,' I said to James.

'That's silly. You're amazing,' he shot back. But I was adamant.

'No,' I said. 'I want a contract but I don't want to be a marquee player.'

'Well, I don't think that's going to be possible,' James replied. 'It looks like the idea of having those extra contracted players is off the table. The only players given contracts will be the two marquees.'

This put me in a real quandary. I was hoping to make some money out of football so that I could put it towards buying my mum a house of her own after all these years of living in a housing commission place. But the only way I could be guaranteed a decent pay packet was to secure a place as a marquee player. I was like, Well, I'm fucked now. First of all, nobody's going to consider me as marquee player because of how I look so I don't want to put myself in that situation. Second, if I try to get a place as a marquee player anyway and get rejected I'll be certain that it was because of how I look, and that will make me feel really bad. So I'm pretty stuffed here. It felt to me like a lose–lose.

Thinking about all this brought me to tears, so I did what I had done so many times before in similar situations: I rang my friend Tegan.

'I don't know what to do,' I said to her. As always, she knew exactly what to say.

'Just go for it. You'll regret it for the rest of your life if you don't. No regrets, Mo. No regrets. Whatever happens is meant to happen.' I put down the phone. I felt the weight of the world on my shoulders and thought, Fuck, I'll have to have a go at it.

I had really enjoyed my time playing for the Western Bulldogs, and I had such a close connection with Susan Alberti, so I was keen to see if they were interested in me being a marquee player for them.

I had a couple of chats with them but it soon became fairly clear that they were more interested in other girls. I think both the Western Bulldogs and Melbourne were placed in a difficult position as they had strong relationships with all of the existing players.

After speaking with the Bulldogs, I received a call from Meg Hutchins, who is Collingwood's women's football operations manager. Meg is a legend of women's footy. She is a six-time All Australian and a long-time star defender with the Eastern Devils in the VWFL. I was stoked to hear from her, and she was really upbeat about Collingwood's interest in me. We arranged to meet at the Magpies' lavish training base at Olympic Park. I decided to take Tegan to the meeting rather than my manager, as she has the knack of keeping me calm at such high-pressure times.

Meg explained how Collingwood was building its women's squad, and how she was going to be on the list as a player as well as running the operations side of the program. She then took me around the club's state-of-the art facilities. For some reason, I felt at home at Collingwood straightaway. I think it might have been the way Meg sold the club as being like one big family. I asked her if it would be okay to bring Vinny to training.

'Not a problem at all,' she immediately replied. When I got home that evening, I rang my manager and told him that I wanted to play for Collingwood.

I became so set on playing for Collingwood that the thought of them not picking me as one of their marquee players kept me awake at night. In late July, however, came the phone call I had been wishing for. The only problem was that I missed it! The person who made the call was Josh Vanderloo, who is the AFL's head of female football and junior development. He left a message saying that he would call back the following day. I was sitting at home on my own watching TV when Josh called back.

'You have been nominated by Collingwood as one of their marquee players,' he told me. I thanked him, then hung up, and started dancing around my lounge room. I'm sure I looked a bit bonkers because I was just so excited. I grabbed my GoPro video recorder and quickly headed over to Mum's place. I turned it on and recorded her reaction when I told her, and this footage was later used on *Australian Story*. Mum was so happy, and we both started crying. When she hugged me I felt like Dad was hugging me as well. It was such an emotional experience. It really felt like both my parents were embracing me at once, just for that moment. When you think of where I have come from in life, it was just breathtaking and mind blowing to have been handed such an opportunity, and I wanted to make the most of it. When she had stopped crying, Mum, in her true Kiwi style, told me the whole thing was 'choice'.

On 27 July, a function was held at AFL House at Melbourne's Etihad Stadium, and I was one of the sixteen women revealed as the marquee players for the inaugural season for the new league. I was seriously nervous, but I decided to ease my nerves by bringing a bit of humour to the occasion. While all sixteen of us were out the back of the stage waiting to be called up, AFL chief executive Gillon McLachlan came in for a quick chat. Some of the girls were sitting there practising what they were going to say on the stage, but I was just mucking around with Collingwood's other marquee player, Emma King. We both have fun-loving personalities, so being serious about the whole thing was never going to work for us.

I told Kingy that I wanted to say something silly to Gill. So when he walked up to us, Kingy said, 'Hey, Gill, Mo wants to ask you a question.' For a couple of seconds, I felt like a turtle that wants to hide in its shell. I didn't think Kingy was actually going to say that to the big boss of the AFL. Gill was like, 'Yeah, what is it, Mo?' I tried to suppress my nerves and replied, 'Now, mate, we need to do something funny when we go out there because we're sick of talking about our journeys. When I walk out, will you dab with me?' Gill gave me a funny look and said, 'What?' Some of the other girls laughed at me, not with me. I'm sure they were thinking, You're an idiot. But, for once, I didn't care.

For those who don't know what the dab is, it's a dance move that apparently originated in the hip-hop scene in the southern part of the United States. To do the move, you raise one arm then look down and cover your face with your other arm. The dab became famous in the sporting world thanks to Cam Newton, who is the Carolina Panthers' quarterback in the NFL. It even crept into cricket over the summer, with Aussie batsman Usman Khwaja doing it after scoring a half-century against Pakistan in a Test match at the Sydney Cricket Ground. West Indian all-rounder Carlos Brathwaite did it five times to celebrate wickets he took playing in the Big Bash for the Sydney Thunder against the Sydney Sixers.

Anyway, Gill had no idea what a dab was, but he was really cool about it. 'Show me,' he said. So I did it for him, and he said, 'Yeah, of course I'll do it.' He stood with us for a couple of minutes practising the move. His arms were all over the place and he kept laughing and saying, 'Am I doing it right?' Just as he was about to walk out of the room, he paused and said, 'It's not bad or evil or, you know, stupid enough to get me into trouble, is it?'

'No way, man!' I said with a giggle. 'It's just a dance move.'

Gill walked off with a chuckle and I glanced around at the other girls. You should have seen some of their faces. They knew I was going to be the star of the show. They had gone from having attitudes like those of high school bullies to being amazed that I was going to dab with the most powerful person in footy.

A couple of the girls even came up to me and said, 'You're not really going to do it, are you?' I shot back at them, 'I don't care what you think. I dab at home with my brothers all the time. If I beat them at footy or basketball, I dab them and it's funny. It's what we do. Why wouldn't I do it with him?'

When my name was called, I walked onto the stage with a big grin. Gill, who was standing behind the lectern, was close to laughing too. When I was within a metre or so of him, I started to dab and he copied in a slightly awkward manner. He chuckled and said, 'Did I get that right?' He then sort of half did it again and said, 'I think I came out the back a bit too hard.' All the journalists and club officials in the crowd were laughing.

Once the formalities had finished, the Collingwood media lady came over to me and said, 'Mo, we've got a problem. Every single media person wants to talk to you and no one else.' For a minute, I lapsed back into my feelings of anxiety.

'Do I look weird? Do they want to talk to me because I look funny?' And straightaway she replied, 'No, it's your personality. They love it. Go and chat to them and be yourself.' I was stoked. 'Awesome,' I said and walked across to the media pack.

Suddenly I was just being myself in front of all these journalists and TV cameras. I felt really comfortable. I made a few wisecracks and the journos chuckled. They all thought it was hilarious and they didn't want to leave. I think some of the other girls were pissed off at me that I had stolen the show, but that didn't worry me one little bit.

That night I was all over the TV news and the various news websites. The *Herald Sun*'s Eliza Sewell was one of those who wrote about the day:

> When Moana Hope was introduced on stage by AFL chief executive Gillon McLachlan as a marquee signing on Wednesday they shared a 'dab'.
>
> The AFL women's league hasn't even started, but Collingwood's newest tattooed forward already has an aura, the star power the famed athletes who usually perform such a celebration dance—like LeBron James—possess.
>
> A media mob soon surrounded the bleached blonde and the story she had to share was equally as powerful as her introduction.

Australian Associated Press also ran a story:

> The inaugural AFL women's league has its first cult figure, with Moana Hope stealing the show as the league's marquee players were announced yesterday.
>
> Hope and AFL chief executive Gillon McLachlan greeted each other on stage in Melbourne with a 'dab' hip-hop dance move as she was confirmed as one of 16 marquee stars for the new league.
>
> She'll play for Collingwood and, similar to Magpies star Dane Swan, her right arm is covered in tattoos.

The Collingwood media team also did an awesome story on me, which appeared on the Magpies' website, next to a photo of me wearing the famous black and white stripes.

> Underneath the tattoo sleeve, the soft voice and the mercurial skills, Moana Hope is a fine footballer …
>
> In 2017, the 28-year-old will become one of Collingwood's first marquee players when she runs out for the Pies in the inaugural Women's AFL competition.

My self-confidence grew enormously after that. I was being applauded for being me, not for trying to be what other people wanted me to be. I was also rapt that by being signed as a marquee player I was guaranteed to receive $25,000 for my first season with Collingwood. I wanted as much of that money as possible to go towards my dream of buying a house for my mum.

In the days after I was confirmed as a marquee player, I went and visited Dad's grave. I wished he could have been part of all these amazing developments, but I knew he would have been so proud of me. I sat next to his grave and had a chat to him in my head, and I felt really at ease with the world.

9

A hundred for the Sharks

BEFORE I COULD start my new footy career as a Collingwood player, I had the rest of the 2016 VWFL season to play out with the St Kilda Sharks. Under the coaching of former North Melbourne and Melbourne player Shaun Smith, a high-flying forward in his day, I had really enjoyed the first half of our VWFL campaign.

Unlike in my previous two seasons with the Sharks, we now had plenty of depth in our forward line, and I received great support from a number of players, including Jasmine Garner, who was later drafted by Collingwood, and Phoebe McWilliams, who will play for Greater Western Sydney in the national league. Still, I was happy to be the star of the show when I could, like the day I kicked ten goals against Bendigo. I was pretty chuffed after that match when Phoebe was quoted in a local newspaper saying that the goal I kicked off the ground while wrestling my opponent was one of the best she had seen.

'I've never played with anyone like her,' Phoebe added. 'She has that X factor ... she can make nothing into something.' I also liked this line from journalist Paul Amy near the end of the story. 'When "Mo" Hope is "on" for the Sharks, the opposition has no hope.'

I played my 200th VWFL game in late April. In quite a coincidence, it was against my old club the Falcons. I kicked three goals but we lost by seventeen points after conceding the first forty points of the game. Then my form improved to the point that I kicked sixteen goals against Knox one afternoon in the middle of the season, then backed that up by booting eleven against Cranbourne. I was just so in the zone during those two games. I literally felt like I had the ball on a string. Those big hauls set me on course to become the first player to top 100 goals in a VWFL season.

The second time we played Knox and Cranbourne I kicked ten goals in both matches, which took my season's tally to ninety-nine in seventeen games. The next week heaps of my family members hired a minibus and travelled down to Seaford on the Mornington Peninsula to see me try to kick that 100th goal in our final home-and-away match of the season. Having my family there pretty much doubled our usual crowd. It was very funny.

I took a mark early, but fell heavily in the process and subsequently missed the set shot. That miss was partly due to being shaken up by the fall and partly due to nerves. Seeing so many members of my family behind the goals made me much more jittery than usual. I desperately wanted to put on a good show for them.

At the twelve-minute mark of the first quarter, I took a mark on the edge of the goal square. My Seaford opponent, Michelle Goodwin, slipped over, so I quickly played on and put my kick right through the middle. I raised my arms in delight as a feeling of relief coursed through my body. My teammates went crazy. They ran from all over the field, and even from the interchange bench, to congratulate me. Then a pile of my brothers and cousins streamed onto the field. They gave me heaps of high-fives and pats on the back before celebrating the occasion with an impromptu rendition of the Haka.

Performing the Haka has always been a big thing for our family. We perform it for any big family occasion, like a funeral, a birthday or even Christmas. My mum was adamant that we all needed to learn the Haka and other traditional dances to keep in touch with our Māori roots. She taught us the moves and bought everyone the right kits to wear. At one stage, she actually brought some of my brothers and nephews together to form a Māori dance group, which performed at functions around Melbourne So seeing the boys performing the Haka out on the footy field in my honour was really special. I think it held up the game for five minutes or so, but no one seemed to care.

A video of my 100th goal and the Haka was later shown on *Australian Story*, and another version later found its way onto *The Age* website. You can still find the second video, which has commentary on the game, if you google it. The commentary never fails to make me smile. 'There's a kick to the top of the square and Moana Hope's taken it!' the commentator yells. 'Plays on, ONE HUNDRED! And they're running onto the ground, they're jumping the fence. Moana Hope, one hundred goals.' Then, when the Haka starts, the commentator isn't sure what's going on. 'I've never seen anything like this,' he says. 'Incredible.'

I ended up kicking five goals all up that day and we won by eighty-three points. I copped a massive drink-bottle shower from all the girls after we sang our victory song: 'Oh when the Sharks go charging in!' I later gave the match ball to Susan Alberti. It was a small way to say thanks for all the support she had given me along the way. Sue later recounted how I came to give her the ball and what the gesture meant:

> Mo came to my apartment to give me the ball that she kicked her hundredth goal with. I didn't know she was coming. I had just sent her an SMS about something, but she didn't answer, which surprised me. Next minute the doorbell goes and it's Mo. She had the ball up the back of her t-shirt. She said, 'We can't repay you for all the support you've given to us. The only way I can say thank you is to give you something that means the most to me, and that's that football I used to kick my hundredth goal.' It was so special. I started crying. That was the most beautiful thing—all the money in the world wouldn't have made me as happy as that football made me. It took my breath away.
>
> I said, 'You really knew how to hide that ball.' She replied, 'When you grow up in Glenroy, you have to know how to do that. Otherwise the other kids will pinch your ball!'
>
> I've since had it put in a glass case and it's in my office. I look at that football and it brings a smile to my face. By the way, I'm going to give it back to her one day. When the time is right, when I know she has a place for it to go, I'll present it back to her. It belongs to her and her family, not to me. But I'm happy to treasure it for now.

The win over Seaford ensured we finished the home-and-away season in second place on the ladder, behind only the Falcons. We thought we were a good chance to win the premiership, which would have been the Sharks' first Division 1 flag since 1999, but the Falcons destroyed us in the second semi-final at the Box Hill Oval. We didn't score in the first three quarters, and we ended up losing 17.11 (113) to 1.1 (7). I hardly touched the ball that afternoon. It was very, very disappointing. We thought we were a decent chance to bounce back in the preliminary final against Melbourne University at North Port Oval, but although I managed to kick two goals, we had another shocker and lost by forty points. It was a sad way to end what had been a great season.

10

Six for the Dogs

THE YEAR 2016 had already been massive for me before the last Western Bulldogs versus Melbourne exhibition game in early September. I had been selected as one of Collingwood's marquee players for the new national women's league and I had become the first player to kick a century of goals in the VWFL. So my last chance to represent the Dogs against the Dees was the icing on the cake.

The lead-up to the game was huge because the Monday night of that week was when the episode of *Australian Story* that featured me and Susan Alberti went to air. I think around a million people watched it, and my phone hardly stopped buzzing all night with people letting me know how much they enjoyed the show. In the following days, people started stopping me in the street and telling me their stories about playing women's footy. Old ladies stopped me, young women stopped me, and my social media accounts were flooded with thousands of new followers. It seemed like people just couldn't get enough of my story. I had so many requests to do radio, television, newspaper and website interviews. In a way it was quite overwhelming, but on the other hand I was thinking, People actually like me, and they don't care how I look.

People really seemed to warm to the parts of the *Australian Story* episode that featured Vinny. A lot of people couldn't believe that I am able to have so much fun with her, that I feel like I can basically ignore her disability when we're together. I think people also respected that I don't look after her because I have to, I do it because I want to.

I ended up going to the Melbourne City Mission and meeting a little old Italian lady who had seen me on the TV program. She wanted to have her photo taken with me. 'You're my biggest inspiration,' she told me. Then she told me her story, of being the full-time carer for her disabled daughter. She also cares for three other family members.

'I quit work years ago and I'm a full-time carer for all four by myself,' she told me. And I was just like, 'You're my inspiration.' So I asked her if I could get a photo with her, and that put a big smile on her face. I still can't believe that my story can provide inspiration to people like her.

◆◆◆

The last women's exhibition game between the Bulldogs and Demons was a big deal because there were no men's AFL matches that weekend. The media really pumped up the game all week, and a crowd of more than 6000 turned up at the Whitten Oval on a Saturday night to see it. The size of the crowd stunned all of us who played in that game. After all, this was not a curtain-raiser to a men's match. All those people travelled to the Whitten Oval just to watch women's footy. As we would later find out, there were many, many more people watching the match from the comfort of their lounge rooms.

I was so much calmer before my last game for the Dogs. I didn't need any Xanax before training or prior to our now-customary pre-match gathering at an inner-city hotel. I felt really at ease. And they way people were around me, I felt like the star of the show. When our bus arrived at the Whitten Oval, I was interviewed by Channel Seven for their coverage. Afterwards I was like, That was nice. It means they care. They didn't pick the talented feminine girl behind me. That's pretty cool.

Thousands of people were already at the ground by the time we ran out for our first warm-up. I could hear young girls screaming my name. I felt a million dollars. Then I went back into the change rooms and did a massive warm-up and said to myself, Fuck, I'm ready to give this a red-hot go. I want to smash it.

When the game started I approached it like I did when I was a little kid running around against the boys. I just let instinct take over. I went out and played the game I loved and got lost in the moment, and it all worked out.

My opponent on the field that day was 37-year-old Cecilia McIntosh, a tough and rugged defender who came to footy after winning a silver medal in javelin at the 2002 Commonwealth Games and then competing in the bobsled at the 2010 Winter Olympics in Vancouver. Cecilia, who played for Melbourne University in the VWFL, is a lot shorter than me but she had given me a good deal of grief when we had played on each other in the past. I always found her to be the type of player I call a 'dirty defender'. This is the type of defender who gets away with things behind play that put you off your game. The umpires never seemed to catch these sorts of moments in the middle of the act. But that was in the VWFL, where we only had two umpires. On this night we had three AFL-standard umpires, so nobody could get away with even half the stuff that went on in games that were not better overseen.

A few minutes into the first quarter, Cecilia hit me in the head and straightaway the umpires awarded me a free kick. I was like, Thank God, finally. It hasn't happened all year but it happens now. I missed the set shot, but that didn't dent my confidence. We were up and going. I kicked another behind, and then late in the second quarter, with us leading by two points, I marked a nice pass from Kaitlyn Ashmore in the right pocket. I was on a tough angle but I went back and put my shot straight through the middle.

'Plenty of hope from there,' the people at home heard Channel Seven commentator Basil Zempilas say on the telecast. 'Good goal.'

Late in the third quarter I still had only one goal to my name, but I soon changed that with one of the favourite pieces of play in my career. A long kick came into our forward line, to a contest between me and Cecilia. As we wrestled about 25 metres out, the ball floated over our heads, so we both quickly doubled back in pursuit of it. Cecilia got back there first. She picked the ball up in the goal square and could have just run it through for a behind, but instead she decided to try to run it out of the Demons' backline. I ran towards her, corralling her near the behind post, so she changed direction, slipped over, then got up and took off again. I gritted my teeth and put in a few quick steps. Once I was within reach of her I lunged forward, wrapped my arms around her, and stripped the ball from her grasp. The Bulldogs supporters went wild as the umpire awarded me a free kick for holding the ball just 10 metres out from goal. That tackle was one of the sweetest things I have done in my life.

I went back and calmly kicked the ball straight over Cecilia's head and through for a goal. I punched the air and jumped into the arms of a few of my teammates. We were fifteen points up and I felt ready to tear the game apart. Two minutes later another long kick came into our forward line. This time the Melbourne defenders had pushed up the ground, leaving me on my own out the back. The kick landed a couple of metres away from me, but I managed to pick it up cleanly. By now I was in the left pocket, not far from the boundary line. I glanced up at the big sticks as Cecilia closed in to within a couple of metres of me. A thought flashed through my head—my instinct game. I kicked these goals every day at the oval with my brothers. Why not now? I placed the ball across my boot and sent a banana kick towards the goals. The crowd roared as it went through, and I ran around the boundary line waving my finger in the air. I'm sure I could see both Dogs and Demons supporters going nuts. I had time to take in the moment and think, This is one of the best moments of my life.

About ninety seconds later, the ball surged into our forward line yet again. Our courageous captain, Stephanie Ciocci, cleaned up Cecilia with a brilliant bump, which cleared a path for me to grab the ball and snap another goal. And my purple patch wasn't over yet. Steph soon won the ball again and belted it forward. The kick looked like it was going to go through for a behind, but it suddenly dropped short and I marked it on my chest about 8 metres from goal. With only a few seconds remaining until three-quarter time, I put my kick right through the middle. My head was spinning as I walked to our huddle. All my teammates were getting around me. I had kicked four goals in the space of five minutes and now had five for the match.

We were up thirty-three points at the last change, and we were never going to lose from there. So the last quarter was such a sweet time. I was able to cap off an amazing night by slotting a 50-metre goal on the run just two minutes before the final siren sounded. I really felt like a superhero at that moment. I just felt like I could do absolutely anything. Lift up the Rialto Towers and carry them a couple of blocks down the street? No worries!

I could not possibly have been happier than I was at the end of the game. The Hampson–Hardeman Cup was being presented for the last time today, as there were to be no more exhibition games. We were getting to take it home, and I had played a key role in the victory. AFL Commission chairman Mike Fitzpatrick came onto the ground to do the presentations and he awarded me the best-on-ground medal. He then directed me towards the microphone. I looked at the crowd and simply said, 'Thanks everybody for coming out. We appreciate it.' Then I walked back to my teammates for another round of hugs and backslapping.

Soon they let all the spectators come down onto the ground and I had hundreds of people crowding around asking me for autographs and to pose for photos with them. I had only signed a few of them when a lady from the Bulldogs told me to leave the field. I told her to get stuffed. This was my chance to give back to the people who had come to watch me. I stood there until I had signed every autograph or posed for a photo with everyone who wanted one. It was a time to savour. I had never felt so good, so accepted, so respected.

Gillon McLachlan walked over and gave me a big hug while I was still out on the ground. I love Gill. He's so lovely. He's been nothing but a gentlemen to me. Susan Alberti also came over and gave me a huge hug. We shared a really special moment. I'm sure she would have loved for me to play for the Bulldogs in the AFLW, but I know that she remains right behind me.

In the days after the game, I had so much interaction with footy fans on social media, while I was walking down the street, just about anywhere. So many of them said the same thing: that they planned on watching five or ten minutes of the game but couldn't turn it off because it was so entertaining and ended up watching the whole thing. So many people told me how they were going nuts when I was kicking my goals. It was extraordinary. A lot of people told me that they found our game more entertaining than the men's footy, because there was less congestion around the ball and very little kicking backwards. I would tell them all to get on board with the women's league in 2017.

'It'll be bigger than the men's one day!' I'd say.

The TV viewer numbers were amazing. On the AFL website they made special mention of this:

> Saturday night's All-Stars women's game between the Western Bulldogs and Melbourne delivered bumper television ratings, with an average of 746,000 viewers (metro and regional) tuning in nationally.
>
> The exhibition match, which was broadcast live by Channel Seven, peaked at 1.05 million viewers and won its timeslot across all key demographics in Melbourne, where it averaged 387,000 viewers.

> It was the largest overall average audience in Melbourne of any game during the 2016 home and away season.
>
> The previous best was the St Kilda–Geelong match in round 14, which drew an average audience of 347,000 viewers, while the Essendon–Richmond Dreamtime at the 'G clash in round 10 nabbed an average of 331,000.
>
> The highly entertaining clash showcased the best women's talent ahead of next year's inaugural national women's league.
>
> Bulldogs forward Moana Hope, who will don the Collingwood guernsey next year, starred with six goals.
>
> AFL chief executive Gillon McLachlan said the higher than expected figures reflected the growing interest in the women's game.
>
> 'These are massive TV numbers, and beyond our expectations. It is thrilling for the AFL and our women players,' McLachlan said in a statement on Sunday.
>
> 'The 6365 crowd at Whitten Oval and the TV viewers watched a fast, skilful and ferocious brand of football, and the women provided a great taste of what's to come when the national league begins in 2017.'
>
> The match also took social media by storm with #AFLWomensGame peaking as Twitter's seventh top trend worldwide on Saturday night.

This was the line that I loved reading over and over again: 'It was the largest overall average audience in Melbourne of any game during the 2016 home and away season.' Ten years before, I could never have imagined that something like this would happen.

The huge ratings numbers ignited a lot of discussion in the media about whether the players in the AFL Women's competition were going to be paid enough. The AFL had offered a deal of $25,000 for marquee players, $10,000 for priority signings and $5000 for other listed players. Health insurance was not part of the deal, and there was no commitment to ensure that the players in the women's competition would be provided with footy boots and runners by their clubs, even though that's what the men's contracts stipulate they are entitled to.

To be honest, I wasn't that fazed by the pay situation. People kept coming up to me and saying, 'Oh, but you should be getting paid much more if you get to play in the AFL Women's.' But the way I looked at it was completely different from how everyone else did. My point was that when the men first started they didn't get that much money. They got bugger all. They had to build things up over time. But even when I said that, people wouldn't listen. They were saying, 'Gillon McLachlan is ripping you off. He's got all these sponsors on board and he's not giving you your share.' Some women even started social media campaigns to try to get more money for the players in the AFL Women's comp.

I appreciated the efforts of those people who wanted to support us and get us more money, but whenever anyone would listen I told them this: the AFL is allowing us to live our dream by bringing the competition forward by three years. Plus, we are only playing eight rounds, plus finals. Plus, right now we are paying fees to play. So we are going from paying fees to getting paid. It's a massive step up.

I asked Nicole Graves her thoughts on the pay issue, and she agrees with me.

The girls don't care about the money. They just want to play footy and be on TV. The money is a bonus. They should be paid, absolutely, but all the media hype about whether they're being paid enough wasn't coming from many of the players. The girls are just rapt that they can play the sport they love at an elite level.

Regardless of the pay debate, my life was going completely haywire—in a good way—since I kicked those six goals for the Bulldogs. The media wanted me to do so many interviews and people wanted me to go to events. There were so many amazing opportunities being presented, I was like, People are asking me to come to their do? Sometimes I was sort of in shock at how lucky I was. I didn't know how to be a celebrity, and the more I went to events and people wanted photos, the more it was like, This is weird, but it makes me feel so happy. I found myself sitting on panels during the AFL finals series with the likes of Cameron Ling and Matthew Richardson, and the next minute I was talking to Nathan Buckley. And they all seemed to like me for who I am. I felt like I was lost in the best possible dream.

In terms of people wanting to know me, I think my appearance on *Australian Story* was just as important as kicking the six goals for the Western Bulldogs. I felt a real sense of acceptance after being on the program because people now knew who the real me was, so they didn't need to judge me any more. They now knew that all my tattoos have deep meanings, that they aren't some bogan accessory.

Although I was getting ready to start training with Collingwood, I considered myself very much a Bulldogs person during the finals. I received so many lovely messages on social media from Dogs supporters who wanted to thank me for playing so well in their jumper. In Grand Final week, I received a message on Instagram from the mother of a young Bulldogs fan. The girl had asked her parents for badges to wear to show her support for the Dogs, but the only faces she wanted on the badges were mine and Susan Alberti's. How cute is that! The mum sent me a video showing the little girl pointing to a picture of me and saying, 'Moana Hope'. Then she would point to a picture of Susan and say, 'Mrs Alberti'.

I ended up getting in contact with the family and I found out they were coming down from Queensland to go to the Grand Final. I met up with them at the Whitten Oval the day after the Bulldogs won the premiership. I told them I was going to give the little girl a footy jumper. They thought it was just going to be any old jumper, but I actually gave her the jumper I wore when I kicked six goals. The kid hugged me like I've never been hugged before. It was such a beautiful moment. So the Bulldogs will always have a place in my heart. I think their supporters are amazing. I can't thank the club enough for helping me turn my life around.

11
A whirlwind

THE TWO MONTHS after the 2016 footy season ended were an absolute maelstrom of activity. So many opportunities came my way, and my manager, James Pitcher, teamed me up with the most amazing group of personal sponsors. I became an ambassador for Melbourne City Mission, Harness Racing Victoria, Moreland City Council's Active Week, Gameday Mouthguards and even the latest *Star Wars* movie. I was invited to speak at business lunches and run footy clinics in places like Warrnambool and Tasmania. I launched a new women's team in the Melbourne suburb of Yarraville and I was even asked to address a group of grade five kids at Melbourne Grammar School, as the teachers felt that my story would inspire them. I felt like a fish out of water at such a prestigious school, but I think my talk went down well. I told the kids about where I had come from but also about the need to be true to yourself and to pursue your dreams, even if that means going against the grain.

Much later I asked James about his recollections of this amazing time:

> The interest in Mo was absolutely staggering. People were ringing me non-stop about her, and sometimes they would say, 'Oh, and what male players do you look after?' I mean, we manage superstars like Gary Ablett and Jack Riewoldt, but Mo was every bit as popular as them. There was seriously a period of time over the summer in which Mo was more popular than our male athletes.
>
> I even had calls from corporations wanting to get her to speak to their executives and employees. Mo ended up addressing people at Lendlease, which is a business that is genuinely trying to increase the number of women in its senior roles. Then I had a call from Macquarie Bank—the 'Millionaires' Factory'—to [ask her to] talk to a team of their bankers in Sydney about her journey and the things she has overcome to get where she is today.

My favourite sponsorship deal of all the ones on offer was with Nike. Remember, I had been the kid so desperate to wear the swoosh that I had drawn it on sweatbands and headbands and t-shirts. Then, suddenly, I was signing a deal with the company that I had been obsessed with all my life. When they sent me a pair of footy boots with the hashtags #hope and #23 (my footy number) on them, I nearly cried. Nike signed me up to be part of their Women's Athlete Group, which features a number of up and coming female athletes. It is an honour to be in it.

I attended many functions during this time where I felt really out of my depth. I remember going to a dinner with all the marquee players and Gillon McLachlan. They sat me next to Gill and I was panicking because I saw that there were three knives and three forks on the table in front of me. I had no idea what was going on. At home when I was growing up, we just had a spoon each. It didn't matter what you were eating, you had to make do with a spoon. So here I am sitting next to Gill, wondering what to do with all the cutlery, and then the waiter comes over and puts my cloth napkin on my lap. I am thinking, What the fuck's this all about—I can do it myself, mate! We never had napkins at our place when I was a kid. So life has become quite bizarre now that I am out of the bubble that I grew up in.

In early November 2016, I was invited to attend Oaks Day at Flemington as a guest of Emirates, the airline that sponsors Collingwood. I went along with Ellie Blackburn, who is one of the Western Bulldogs' marquee players. I was quite anxious beforehand, particularly about what to wear. I knew all the women would be wearing expensive dresses, but I didn't want to put myself in clothing that I wasn't going to feel comfortable wearing. In the end, I decided to rock up in a pair of $40 grey pants from Myer, along with a cheap jacket-and-hat combo—oh, and the pearls that Susan Alberti gave me. On my way to the races I sent out a tweet saying, 'When you're the only girl at the races not wearing a dress but rocking some pearls—just me . . .'

I hoped that the people in the Emirates marquee would accept me for who I was, although I was a bit worried about getting knocked back at the door because I didn't look like the other girls and wasn't wearing any make-up. The thing is, I have been stopped from getting into clubs over the years because I wasn't wearing a dress and heels. So when I got to the door and the person checking the wristbands smiled and waved me through, I was like, Wow, they accept me—this is cool.

I didn't know what to expect. I just thought it was going to be like a little tent, and I'd hang out with some mates. As soon as I walked in the entrance, I was like, Holy shit. It was like the epic party scene in the movie *The Great Gatsby*. I felt really intimidated. Everyone in there was a VIP or a celebrity—someone who had a big-shot reputation. And then there was me. The chick from Glenroy who plays footy. I couldn't stop thinking, You've got to be fucking kidding me. How did I get invited to this place? It was so intense that I went straight to the bar and knocked back a couple of calming drinks.

All the women and all the men looked amazing. Of course, the women were in these beautiful dresses, and they had headpieces the size of the room, and some had chains of diamonds coming down over their faces and, for a short time, I found myself wondering, Do they think I missed the memo about the dress code? Once I might have suffered a full-on panic attack in a situation like this, but now I had come full circle and didn't care what anyone thought about me. I was being myself, and I was proud of that.

As I looked around, I thought, I'm here because I'm a footballer and you're possibly here because you own half of Melbourne. But I didn't turn my nose up at them and think they were bad people for living in this glamorous world, as I once would have. The thing is, most of them were lovely, and some of them were seriously cool people.

The most amazing person I met was Turia Pitt, who suffered burns to 65 per cent of her body when she became trapped in a bushfire while running an ultra marathon in Western Australia in 2011. Since then, Turia has become known around the world for her positive attitude. Her face was disfigured by the burns, but she has become a crusader for the idea that you shouldn't judge a book by its cover. She may no longer look like the model she once was, but she is an amazingly beautiful person. Turia has also made a huge impact through her efforts to raise money to help burns victims in the developing world. And as if all that isn't inspirational enough, prior to Oaks Day she had completed the Hawaiian Ironman competition, which involves a 3.8-kilometre swim, a 180-kilometre bike ride and a 42.2-kilometre run. She had finished the entire event, all three courses, in just fourteen hours.

I first saw Turia while I was waiting to be served at the bar. I thought, Oh my God, I really want to meet you. I was too shy to go up to her, but the next minute she was patting me on the shoulder because she wanted to meet me. She had watched the episode of *Australian Story* and she said to me, 'I'm a big fan of yours.' I turned to her and replied, 'Seriously, I just play footy. You are out there saving the world. I am a massive fan of yours.'

A bit later I met 'Magnolia' Maminydjama Maymuru, who was the first Indigenous model to represent the Northern Territory in the Miss World Australia competition and is now the face of Melbourne's Chadstone shopping centre. She was just blown away by me, because she played football growing up even though now she's this big-time model. I couldn't quite believe it when she asked to get a photo with me. I remember joking with her, 'You're the famous person and you're asking me for a photo? It's just weird!'

My only disappointment was that I had been hoping to meet Michelle Payne, but in the end it didn't happen. I can really relate to the way that Michelle has risen to the pinnacle of her sport despite her humble beginnings. I thought her win on Prince of Penzance in the 2015 Melbourne Cup was one of the most amazing sporting achievements I had ever seen. But the thing I love the most about Michelle is the way she cares so much for her brother, Stevie, who has Down's syndrome. Michelle doesn't treat him any differently from anyone else, and that's how it should be. Like my sister Vinny, Stevie has so much to offer the world. I also admire the way Michelle has to fight for everything she gets in such a male-dominated sport. And even though she has achieved so much, she still seems to be down to earth, really normal.

Before my day in the Emirates marquee was over, a reporter and photographer from *The Age* had bailed me up for an interview and a photo, then Channel Seven had asked to interview me as part of their telecast of the races. I remember saying to the people from Channel Seven, 'Do you know who's in this tent? Jen Hawkins is in there, Turia Pitt is in there, stacks of famous footballers are in there, surely you don't want to interview me?' But they did. It was all very surreal.

A few times I had to go outside the marquee and just gather my thoughts for a while. But people kept coming up to me and asking for photos or just to say hi. Here I was, dressed in cheap clothes and looking like a bloke, and everyone thought I was great. It made me feel so good inside. I posted a photo of my outfit on Instagram and the response was amazing. People loved that I had gone to such a glamorous event and had just been myself. I received messages from a lot of young girls saying that I was such a great role model for them. I had shown them that you don't have to do what everyone else is doing. I was very pleased that I could help others be themselves.

I try to get back to everybody who messages me something positive on social media. I think that if they have taken the time to send a message, then I should take the time to acknowledge them. I realise now how many of the people who message me see me as a role model, and responding to their messages is a way that I can give back to them and encourage them. So many of the young women who message me are inspired that I have kept playing footy, despite the amount of people who look down on us, and still think it's just a bunch of butch lesbians involved in the women's side of the game, instead of the reality, which is that we are a wide range of women from many walks of life. Girls have the right to feel good about playing footy, and that is something I can now help others with. I know it means a lot to many of them if I even just take a few seconds to write, 'Thanks for your support', when they get in touch.

Around the time that I went to Oaks Day, a young girl sent me a message on Instagram that read, 'You're my inspiration.' I looked at her Instagram feed and saw that she played football, so I wrote back, 'I see you play footy, that's awesome, keep at it.' Her mum then messaged me on Facebook. It was an amazing message and it went something like this: 'I just want you to know that what you've done today has changed my daughter's life.' The mum wrote at length about how her daughter had suffered depression and other mental health problems, and had thought about suicide. She had watched her daughter read my message and had been amazed at the impact it had. She wrote to me that she had never seen her daughter smile so much for such a long time. Her daughter is now in a much better place. She is not worrying about what people at her school think about her and she is really getting stuck into playing footy and trying to reach the AFL.

To be able to have an impact on people like this is an amazing gift. When I think back to when I was that girl's age, I would have given anything to have a role model who contacted me to say that playing footy was a cool thing for girls to do. But I didn't have that. I think I might have written letters to some of my idols, but of course there was no social media back then, so it was much harder to get a reply. It's so much easier to communicate with people now, so the least I can do for the young women looking up to me is to reply to their messages. I'm not saying I'm responsible for changing their lives. Even with the girl I mentioned before, I'm sure there are a lot of people close to her doing some great things to get her back on track. I don't want to overstate what I can do for people. But when people send me positive messages it gives me such a lift, so I know that to send messages back the other way can be just as powerful. If I can help people be themselves, and not feel pressure to conform to how other people think they should be, then I want to make sure I put in the time and effort to do just that.

The people who send me messages probably don't realise just how much they also inspire me. I had a message from a bunch of guys who started a group for Movember, the annual fundraising event to raise awareness of men's health issues. There were fifteen of them and they didn't know what to call their group. But they were so in awe of me and my story, they called it the Mo Hope Group. I thought that was pretty good, and witty. So I jumped online, donated to their group and started sharing their story on social media. For me, doing things like that is much more important than going to glamorous events and meeting famous people. Don't get me wrong, I love getting the chance to do these other things and I am very appreciative of all that has come my way. But giving back to the community and sharing my good fortune with others means so much more to me.

In late 2016, I had a message from a lady in Tasmania, whose daughter was a big fan of mine. So when I went down there to do a footy clinic, I met up with them and had a kick of the footy with the daughter. She was so thankful and it made me feel so good. When I was messaging the mother whose daughter had depression, I straightaway asked if they were in Melbourne, because I thought I could maybe go and kick the footy with the daughter once a week or something like that. It turns out that they live in Western Australia, so I sent her a footy jumper and have promised to meet up with them when I can. Making connections with others is where my power lies. That's where I can make the biggest difference to people's lives, particularly young women who are shy and insecure, like I was at their age.

12

Welcome to the Magpies

I HAVE LOVED THE Collingwood Football Club from the moment I first set foot in the place. The club felt like a huge family to me then and nothing has changed that feeling. The thing I love the most about Collingwood is that no one at the club has ever asked me to change. No one has asked me to cover my tattoos or try to make my hair look prettier. Quite the opposite, in fact. I knew the Collingwood people loved the way I look when they had my picture down the side of their website over summer, with my tattoos in full view. No matter what page you clicked, my picture remained there on the side, which made me so pleased.

In the days after I was announced as one of Collingwood's marquee players for the AFL Women's league, everybody, from the staff to the board to the male players and the members of the Magpies' new netball team, was so welcoming. Collingwood president Eddie McGuire was probably the most hospitable of them all. Eddie is a real cool dude. He's really lovely. Eddie and I grew up a couple of hundred metres away from each other, so I get where he's coming from. It's the same sort of feeling I have with Susan Alberti. None of us got anything handed to us on a silver platter. Eddie is doing so many great things for women's footy and netball, and seeing him in action at Collingwood's Christmas lunch for the homeless was mind blowing, he's just so great.

To backtrack a little, I was scared when I first met Eddie. It was at a function to launch Collingwood's women's team and there were 600 people there. I'll never forget the way Eddie put me at ease when he introduced himself. He just smiled and said, 'Welcome to the club. We're so happy to have you here.' And I was like, Okay, this is amazing. He then took me aside for a chat. He was so keen to know a bit more about my story and the journey that had led me to the Magpies.

After we had chatted for a while, Eddie said, 'I'm going to get you up on stage.' Once I was up in front of the crowd, he gave me a gift to welcome me to the club and started asking me questions. He made the whole thing a great deal of fun. He kept saying things like, 'We love your tattoos. We just love your tatts. You're the new Dane Swan!' Eddie loved the fact that I had grown up in the northern suburbs, like him, and he kept pumping me up by saying, 'You're an amazing footballer, we love you, we're excited to have you here.' When I returned to my table, I had such a warm feeling inside. I kept thinking, You accept me for who I am.

In the days after that function, I did a lot of media stuff. The staff who helped me with those appearances were so encouraging and accepting of me. They would say, 'Mo, just go out there and be yourself'. Then, after I had finished the interviews, they would say, 'Mo, awesome interview, loved it. Don't you go changing the way you are.' So many other people were similarly friendly. David Emerson, who is Collingwood's director of operations, was brilliant. He's basically in charge of just about everything at the club, and yet he had so much time for me. So, everyone at Collingwood supported me so much that it made me want to try even harder to be the best footballer I could be.

The Magpies' other marquee player, Emma King, and I became really good friends during those few weeks before the club drafted in the rest of its squad. Kingy is from Western Australia and would have been offered a spot on Fremantle's list but decided she was keen to move across the country and sample the Victorian lifestyle. She is very tall and people always assume she has come to footy from basketball. But, as she is only too happy to admit, she can't play basketball to save herself! She actually has a background in surf life saving, having grown up near the beach. I had played alongside Kingy for the Western Bulldogs on a couple of occasions, but we didn't really hit it off until we arrived at Collingwood. Kingy's take on how our friendship has developed is that:

> When I first met her, when we played for the Western Bulldogs together, Mo scared the shit out of me. I was intimidated by her tattoos and she seemed to have a big persona around the people she knew well. So I didn't really talk to her the first time we played for the Dogs, then I got to know her when we played together the second time. I found out she's like the nicest person you'll ever meet. She's so kind-hearted and wants everyone to succeed.
>
> I never had any doubts about her talent as a footy player. I mean, when she kicked those six goals for the Bulldogs

it was a ridiculous performance. I have never seen another female play footy like her. She seems to know where the ball is going to go. During games, you find yourself thinking she's out of position and won't get the ball, but the next minute she's kicked a goal and you're like, wow.

When I came over to Collingwood, I was a bit iffy on how we would get on because we hadn't spent much time together before, yet we were going to have to do a lot of appearances together as marquee players. I sort of thought anything could happen, but we just hit it off straightaway. We have a very similar sense of humour, which helps. Neither of us take ourselves too seriously. We both love taking the piss out of each other.

I think Mo is the kind of character that footy fans have been crying out for. She has such a great story and she's so real, if you know what I mean. Everyone can relate to her. And she now has such belief in herself. She told me when I first came over and started doing media, 'They want you to be yourself, so be yourself'. And that's probably some of the best advice I've had. Mo makes sure she gives everyone that same advice: 'Just be yourself, don't try to be someone you're not.' That's something that is making Mo a real leader in women's footy.

Kingy is very funny. When I was doing all that media about dabbing Gill and being a marquee player, she kept stirring me about how famous I was. She thought it was hilarious when we went out to a club one night and everyone kept coming up to me and asking for photos. Kingy jokes that I get mobbed everywhere I go:

> Everywhere we go, people are like, 'Can I get a photo with you, Mo?' I find myself just standing there watching it all unfold. I'm like Mo's handbag. None of them ever know who I am, so I offer to take the photos. When I go home to Western Australia, I tell people how famous Mo is. They're like, whatever. I say to them, 'Honestly, she is so famous.' It's always funny when people fan-girl her and I'm like, 'Hey, I hang out with her every day. She's not that great!'

Sometimes people ask me if I feel famous. But I don't. Not at all. Although Vinny tells me every single day that I'm famous, which is so cute. In all seriousness, I never look at it like people are stopping me—they're stopping the girl that plays football. Women's football is the reason why I'm being recognised. For me, having come from a position where people always thought I was weird because I was a girl who wanted to play footy, it's an incredible thing that people want to be seen with a female footballer. That's the most exciting thing: people are noticing women's football. That's the biggest positive.

Kingy and I spent a lot of time together in the months after we became Collingwood's marquee players, as we had to attend a lot of functions and launches. One of them was the apparel launch for the AFL Women's competition. All the apparel is being made by Cotton On, under its sports brand, COAR, and it is great stuff. The launch was held in a big warehouse in the Melbourne suburb of Kensington. We had to pose for a lot of photos, and some of the girls from the other clubs were really serious about it. They were so stiff that the photographers had to tell them to loosen up a bit. In contrast, Kingy and I mucked around so much that the photographers eventually said, 'Can you just be sensible for a minute so we can take a normal photo?' We tried to be as serious as we could be, but we just ended up looking goofy. We thought the whole thing was hilarious.

The environment Kingy and I have walked into at Collingwood is remarkable. The club now has four sporting teams working out of the Holden Centre—the AFL men's footy team, the AFL women's footy team, the VFL footy team and the Super Netball team—and the players from each set-up get along really well. When you walk through the corridors of the Holden Centre, people go up to each other and say, 'Oh, you're a women's football player. That's cool.' I have met the most impressive array of athletes at the club, from star AFL footballers to star netballers—Collingwood's Super Netball franchise has seven Australian Diamonds players in its squad—and I have learned something from all of them.

I have been so impressed by the support that the male Collingwood players have given us. Particularly during our early weeks around the club, they were all really kind, although I would have to say that footballer Adam Treloar impressed me the most. He is such a gentleman. He's a beautiful man and I hope one day he captains for Collingwood. After I kicked six goals for the Bulldogs in the last exhibition match, he sent me a message: 'What a great game. You're a legend. Can't wait to see you in black and white.' And I was like, Oh my God, there's a Collingwood player messaging me.

The Collingwood people are also so accepting of Vinny when I bring her along to functions or to the gym. I'm very protective of Vinny and I'm always very alert to the way people look at her and treat her. When we go shopping together, we often come across so many nasty people who point at her and laugh about the way she looks and call her retarded—I fucking hate that word. It's like I'm walking along with an alien beside me, and it makes me so upset. But when I took Vinny to Collingwood the first time, everyone at the club was so happy to meet her. They accepted her for who she was not what she wasn't, just like they accepted me from the start. I can't describe how significant that is.

We started our official pre-season training on 22 November, although I had done plenty of sessions in the gym before then. There had been some very exciting big-picture developments in the lead-up to us hitting the track, including an even better pay deal for the AFL Women's players than had originally been promised. This is the press release that was sent out by the AFL on the day that the deal was announced:

> The AFL and AFL Players' Association have reached an agreement on the remuneration package NAB AFL Women's players will receive in the 2017 and 2018 seasons.
>
> In 2017, marquee players will receive a financial package of $27,000 (inclusive of $10,000 for their marketing and ambassadorial role), the priority players $12,000 and the remaining listed players $8,500 for the seven match (plus Grand Final) season.
>
> The packages will increase to $27,946, $12,846 and $9,276 respectively in 2018.
>
> The AFL Commission recently approved an increase to the initial remuneration package offered to all players to contribute to the cost of the required level of private health insurance, as well as further raising the base level payment.

In addition to the package, the NAB AFL Women's players will receive:

- Football boots and runners
- Travel allowance when playing interstate
- Income protection insurance
- Coverage for out-of-pocket medical expenses for the 52 weeks post contract
- An allowance to pay for a carer when travelling interstate in cases where a player has a child under 12 months.

I was always pretty happy with the AFL's original pay offer. But I'm not complaining about the fact they've improved it. A lot of the credit for the increase needs to go to the AFL Players' Association. Even before the draft was held to distribute the talent for the women's league, the AFLPA worked really hard to get all the best female players in Australia on the same page. The people from the AFLPA were clear that we needed to be really strong when we negotiated our first pay deal, otherwise the AFL would walk all over us forever. The AFLPA made sure they had all the marquee players on board first, then we were able to spread the word to get the rest of the players to sign up. We would tell the players at our clubs, 'Pay attention to what they're saying, because they're doing it for the betterment of everyone in the league.' We were able to get the result we were after.

What I know is that once the AFL Women's competition becomes more popular, the pay for the players involved will improve. I'm confident that in time we will get to the position of strength that Australia's best female cricketers now find themselves in. They struck a new pay deal with Cricket Australia in April

2016 that means players who represent the Southern Stars (our women's national team) on a consistent basis and play in the women's Big Bash League will be able to earn more than $100,000 a year.

For me, playing sport has never been about money. It has been about doing something that I love. Even now, when I am able to earn money through playing footy, it's not about making myself rich. I just want to help my family, especially my mum.

The first pre-season with Collingwood, under senior coach Wayne Siekman, we started off with a serious workload. The whole training program was tailored around the fact that most of women in the squad were working full-time, so we trained in the evenings, with most sessions starting around 6.30 pm and lasting for a couple of hours—every player in the AFL Women's competition is contracted to spend nine hours per week at their club. A few weeks in, however, the coaches sat us down in groups and asked us for feedback on how we were going. The consistent feedback was that all the girls were exhausted. Most of us weren't eating enough because we were so busy with work and all the other things we do outside of footy. In my case, I am, of course, up every day at 3 or 4 am to start work. I have to sort out where I need to send my people, and then make sure they are all on the road before the peak-hour traffic starts to build. Then I get Vinny ready and take her to the place she is looked after during the day. For the rest of the day I find myself juggling traffic management issues and requests to do stuff for Collingwood or the AFL. By the time I get to training, I am usually hungry and tired.

I'm certainly not the only player on Collingwood's list who leads a very hectic life. It's an issue for most of us. As a result, we would come to training and try to get up and about, but it was really hard because we were so tired. The coaches were fantastic. They listened to all our concerns and made a number of changes to our program. The club came to the party by putting on dinner for all of us after every training session. I hug the coaches every mealtime—free food is the way to my heart! I have so much going on in my life that I never have enough time to eat properly, and I'm sure a lot of the other girls are in the same boat. I'm just so busy that I forget to eat, which is the worst thing for my body, and something I'm trying to change. Having the club organising those three meals a week is so nice, because they are three meals a week that I might not have eaten. So that's why I've got so much respect for the club and our coaches, because they really went above and beyond to listen and then look after all us girls.

I actually had to do a lot of cross-training work in late November and early December because I was experiencing pain in my lower back. But the Collingwood physios got on top of the condition in the end, and I was able to join in some of the footy drills with my teammates prior to Christmas. Funnily enough, the milestone was overshadowed by all the stuff happening off the field.

First, one of Collingwood's major sponsors, Holden, gave me a brand-new car, an electric blue Holden Trax. The deal with the car is that I get it for free while I am a contracted player at Collingwood. When my manager, James Pitcher, told me I was getting the car I was overwhelmed. I had never had a new car before, so I felt so elated when they handed it over to me. I drove it straight to Mum's house and everyone who was there at the time came out and looked at it. I don't think any of them had been near a new car before. They were all saying, 'Let me take it for a drive,' but I was like, 'It's a brand-new car, you're not driving it.' I feel quite special to have received it. In fact, I'm beyond grateful. They could have given me a car from 1942 and I still would have driven it because it gets you from A to B. But it's a brand spanker, and being an SUV it's so nice and big. Vinny loves it because there's more legroom in the back compared with the cars I have had in the past.

Not long after I received my new car, I was featured in a *Herald Sun* story by Eliza Sewell, which really pumped my tyres up:

> Moana Hope is one of the hottest properties in football.
>
> With an autobiography due out next year and talk of a kids book series too, the rise and rise of the heavily tattooed girl from Glenroy continues.
>
> Certainly when the Collingwood forward's new blue Holden rolled into her street, the reality of a new life hit home.
>
> 'This is how my family is when someone gets a new car (doesn't happen often or ever so we soak up them moments side by side),' Hope posted on Instagram with a photo of her siblings eyeing off her new wheels.
>
> The marquee Magpie hasn't played a game in black and white but after opening up on ABC's *Australian Story* in August and then kicking six goals in the AFL's exhibition game on September 3—the flame was lit.
>
> Hope is now the face of a mouthguard, hosts clinics, has ambassador roles (with Harness Racing Victoria and charity Melbourne City Mission) and is in heavy demand for appearances.
>
> Next year we'll see her on a women's footy TV show and hear her on Gold FM.

> But it's her Nike sponsorship, complete with electric blue boots carrying her number (No. 23, of course) and name, that shows how far the 28-year-old has come.
>
> 'She didn't have the luxury of being able to buy Nike when she was a kid,' manager James Pitcher told the *Herald Sun*.
>
> 'They used to buy stuff ... like sweat bands and draw the swooshes on.'
>
> The interest in his client is such that Pitcher is having about four meetings a week to discuss opportunities.

My teammates—Kingy in particular—stirred me up a lot about the article. We have a fines system, whereby any player who appears in the media has to put a couple of dollars in a jar. After that article was published in the *Herald Sun*, Kingy said to me, 'Mo, just put $50 in the jar at the start of each week!' I think I'll have to ask Eddie McGuire for access to his spare change drawer to meet the cost of all these fines.

I am rapt that people like Emily Woods continue to follow my progress from afar. I was able to chat to Emily around Christmas time and it was awesome to hear how thrilled she is by the way that women's footy is taking the world by storm. Emily has viewed my progress closely, and says:

> Watching Mo in those exhibition matches was just great, and then I watched the *Australian Story* episode and I thought it was a fantastic story, but it seemed to have put a lot of pressure on the last exhibition match. And then when she came out and kicked those six goals, it was amazing. I couldn't help but think that she can clearly handle the pressure now.

When I think back to her younger days, she obviously used to represent Victoria and all that sort of stuff, but she was never the standout player or the face of women's footy or the one that you'd go to a footy game to watch. Daisy Pearce was that kind of player. But Mo is now someone who has all the attributes to be the face of the game. You don't see many great full-forwards in the men's game anymore, let alone full-forwards who can kick a hundred goals in a season, so she is a real drawcard. To see her kick a hundred goals for the St Kilda Sharks was amazing.

Although I'm an Essendon supporter, I'm rapt that she has been recruited by Collingwood. She's almost taken over Dane Swan's role as the tattooed cult hero. I was in Melbourne over Christmas visiting the family and I opened up the *Herald Sun* and saw the full-page spread on her. I couldn't help but be happy for her. Mo does so much for charities and for her sister and her family as a whole. She's such a humble kid, but she's an extraordinary person at the same time.

My mate Nicole Graves is another great friend who continues to support me from afar:

I'm so chuffed that Mo has become hot property. She deserves it, because she's got a good heart and she is a fantastic story. I'm glad the media has jumped on someone who's a bit off-centre and not the same boring, perfect type of person that dominates the footy coverage nowadays.

The most important thing about the AFL Women's competition is that we have so many different characters from such diverse backgrounds. It's nice to see that women's footy has become a game for everyone. You don't have to be a university graduate or to have a perfect image to be accepted in the game. It's a wonderful thing. Mo Hope and Daisy Pearce are both elite at what they can do on the footy field and they are both leaders in their own way, but they are completely different people. Yet both of them are being promoted as key members of the sport at the elite level.

I also remain extremely close to Sue Alberti, and she continues to support me in more ways than one:

Mo feels inadequate in many ways, given she hasn't done a lot of schooling and probably doesn't read and write as well as many people. But every time I speak to her I say, 'Mo, don't let that worry you.' I didn't have a tertiary education and I've managed. I've believed in myself, I've surrounded myself with people who are smarter than me, I've learned from them and gained knowledge from them. I've had lots of downs as well as ups, but I think I'm helping her believe in herself that she's going to be okay. I think she knows I've accepted her and I'm not afraid to be out with her, to be seen with her, to be talking to her. We love one another. She's like a daughter to me now. I really love her and I want to help her, if she wants me to. I want to mentor her and give her that confidence that she desperately needs.

I love all the young women who play footy. They're like my family. I don't care who they play for. I just want them to be successful. You can overcome just about anything if you really put your mind to it. That's the way I look at life. The bigger the challenge the harder I work. I've always had that philosophy. I'm not sure whether Mo has exactly the same attitude, but look what she's achieved in the face of such adversity. She can help other young girls aspire to be the best, if they really want to. She will be able to leave a legacy that says to young girls, 'If you have a dream, if you aspire to do something great, you can do it.'

No matter what happens from here, I will never forget the people who helped me get to the AFL.

13
Across the ditch

I HAD SOME TIME away from footy in the middle of preseason when I travelled to New Zealand for the first time. I'm extremely proud of my Māori heritage, so it had long been an ambition of mine to go there. The reason for the trip was an emotional one: we went to see the unveiling of my grandfather's tombstone. Despite her various health problems, Mum garnered the strength to come along, which was so important as it was her father who we were honouring. All of my thirteen brothers and sisters came as well, which meant it was like a big family reunion. It was the first time we had ever been overseas as a family. It was also the first holiday I had taken in three years, so I was really hanging out for it.

The trip was incredibly important for Mum. She had waited so long to take her kids back home for the first time and to meet her huge extended family. The trip was also really important for me. It might turn out to be the first and last international trip I get to do with my mum, so it was something I wanted to cherish every day we were there.

My siblings saved up their money for more than a year so they could come on the trip. They would give Mum fifty or a hundred bucks a week out of their pay. She put the money aside and when she had enough for the airfares, she booked them. Similarly, when there was enough money for the accommodation, she booked it.

Because of everything that is going on in my life, with footy and media appearances and my new car and stuff like that, my brothers and sisters all think I'm rich. So they were trying to scam money out of me to pay for things on the trip. They were like, 'Oh, I'm broke, please pay for this' or, 'Moana, please pay for my dinner.' I had no problem telling them to get stuffed sometimes. But I wasn't being nasty to them when I did that. Everyone in my family knows that I care deeply about them, and they all know that I am putting most of my money towards caring for Mum.

Even if I become very successful in my life from here, and end up in a comfortable financial position, I will never be a person who just keeps it all for myself. Sharing my good fortune with my family is so important to me. I want my family to experience what I am experiencing. Even though I'm by no means rich right now, I helped everyone out where I could on the trip to New Zealand by shouting them a few dinners and things like that. The other thing I am perennially conscious of is never putting any of my siblings down. I never go around saying, 'Hey, I've got money' or, 'I earn good money from work but you don't' or, 'I support Mum and Vinny and you don't, or think less of them. My family are my family and I will help them no matter what. Helping them also makes me feel close to Dad. I feel like I have got to a point in life where I can continue his role in terms of supporting the family. That might sound weird, but I feel like I can do what he would have done to support everyone if he were still here.

I sometimes get asked if I feel a lot of pressure to support my family, or if I'm feeling like I am carrying my family around on my back. People ask if being the main breadwinner in such a big clan is stressful. Well, it can be, don't worry about that. But, to me, your family are the most important people in your life. And no matter what happens in my life, with football or work or things like that, my family will always be there. Funnily enough, the pressure to get somewhere in life, to help my family, actually drives me. It makes me get out of bed each morning. In that way, it's a good thing.

In New Zealand we travelled to my mum's hometown of Kaitaia, which is located near the top of the North Island. It is an area that is steeped in Māori history and still has a large Māori population. My grandfather, whose name was Joseph, had been a chief, so the service for the unveiling of his tombstone was very important in the local community. The tombstone unveiling is called *Hura Kohatu* in the Māori language and it is held around one year after the person has died. It is the last time that a family shares its sorrow in public.

It was really amazing to experience the unveiling ceremony, and I found all the customs and traditions we had to adhere to very interesting. As we left the cemetery, for example, we had to wash our hands and sprinkle some water on ourselves so that we didn't take any bad spirits away with us. We also got to experience a service in a marae, which is a Māori church. The marae that we visited was started by my great-great-grandparents and their pictures were on the wall.

The people who run the marae were able to tell us about the customs that featured in my grandfather's funeral. When someone passes away in this part of New Zealand, the family sleep in the marae beside the casket for three nights. People come and visit the casket to say goodbye to the person during the day. It's all very different from what happens in most of Australia when people die.

We had some very deep spiritual moments in New Zealand, but we also had a lot of fun. Being together as a family gave us the chance to muck around like we did when we were kids. Every morning we would knock on each other's doors and yell out, 'Get up, you lazy shit,' or some kind of banter like that. We were always playing pranks on each other. We tried to get out and about and see the region around Kaitaia, and this created more amusement. One day we hired quad bikes and rode along the beach. We had a four-wheel drive following us on the beach and I asked them if I could drive the car for a bit. I managed to get it bogged. Idiot!

Some nights we just sat in one of our rooms and played games until one o'clock in the morning. We were carrying on like we were still children, making each other laugh and taking the piss out of each other. If you look in depth at the lives that my siblings are leading, there are plenty of issues they face. But for that time in New Zealand we felt like carefree kids again, which was a truly great thing.

Being true to who you are

My trip to New Zealand put me in a great headspace to have a really strong finish to my pre-season training back at Collingwood. I worked super hard on the track and in the gym throughout January, and thanks to the support I received from all of the club's fitness staff—Michelle, a physio, in particular—I got so fit that I felt like I was seventeen again. I kept thinking, I wish I wasn't twenty-eight. I wish this was all happening ten years ago.

My favourite memory of training in January was completing my first full session on the track. I achieved this milestone on 10 January, just two weeks before our Australia Day practice match against the Western Bulldogs. I was so excited in the lead-up to that session that I arrived at the club three hours early. I just couldn't wait to get out there with my teammates. There were a few funny moments early in the session, because five minutes in I found myself gasping for air. I was thinking, Am I really unfit or are these guys over-the-top fit? Do you know that feeling when you're overexcited and happy, and you literally can't breathe? That's what it was like. So it took me about half an hour to get into the groove on the track and then suddenly everything felt right. I was like, Yeah, this is it. I was so happy. I seriously couldn't wipe the smile off my face.

When we took on the Dogs on Australia Day, the weather was great and quite a few people turned up to see the match. I kicked one goal as we lost to one of the premiership favourites by only a few points. However, it was a frustrating game at times, as it was often quite congested, with lots of players crowded around the ball. I'm not exactly sure what caused this, but I think the nerves among the players probably played a part. A lot of players seemed a bit scared to take a risk and move the ball out into the open. This was understandable in a way, given we were all playing for spots in our clubs' first official games.

Post-match, our coach spoke about maybe introducing some new rules into the women's competition to prevent so many players from crowding around the ball. He suggested that a good rule would be to make sure that each team has two of their players inside their forward and defensive 50-metre arcs at all times. I think this would open the game up in a big way. It would certainly help me as a forward. There's nothing worse than having heaps of players dropping back in front of me and taking away my space to lead. And, when you think about it, the women's game needs to be all about entertainment. No one wants to come along to games and see defensive tactics that lead to a final score of two goals versus one goal. Everyone wants to see exciting play with forwards taking big marks. I know I'm biased, given I'm a key forward, but I have no doubt that when people go to the footy they want to see lots of goals.

After our loss to the Bulldogs, it was time for the real stuff—the official AFL Women's league games—to start. It was time for the dreams of every woman who has ever played our great game to come true. The lead-up to our historic clash with Carlton at Princes Park (or Ikon Park, to use its commercial name) was something of a blur. I did so many media appearances that I lost count of them. In fact, I did so much media that finding the time for training was a battle. But that period of time was so much fun. It was amazing to see women's footy all over the newspapers and the nightly news. I was rapt to feature in a documentary called *League Of Her Own*, which had award-winning producer Nicole Minchin and sports journalist and author Angela Pippos on board, and detailed the long struggle to bring women's footy into the mainstream. I was rapt to see people like Debbie Lee and Lisa Hardeman featured. They were among the true pioneers of women's footy. People like me owe them a great deal of thanks and respect.

◆◆◆

As I look back to the beginning of the AFL women's competition, it feels like we had a dream run. It was such a positive start—the way the public got on board, the way the media took it on, the way the AFL backed it. Those first weeks of training and the start of the competition, it felt like so many dreams were being realised, not only for the girls playing, but for all those watching on the sidelines.

The most incredible part of the AFL women's season, and the thing that I will never forget, is the love and enthusiasm for us in the community, even from people who have not previously followed AFL. The highlight for me of the entire season was when people cried after the first bounce. I had shocking nerves, as I mentioned earlier, but the roars from the crowd just kept us all going and we felt like we were playing on a cloud. That game was a blur of nerves and excitement. It took until the second game for me to find my rhythm. I had started to realise that each game was going to be completely different, and that I could never anticipate how a team would play. That you could never really know what your opposition would be like, and once you felt you had a handle on them, they could change direction. I've played a lot of footy in my life, but playing AFL is something completely different.

It's been an incredible ride. I still have to pinch myself every time I think about the opportunity I have been given to play AFLW. It has been amazing what these women in the competition have been able to achieve in the first year, especially off the back of a limited preparation and us playing together for the first time. For the girls who are starting out playing footy now, there will one day be a full-time AFL women's league, and they will get paid to play footy all year, however for the current women playing, we are just so excited at being given this opportunity. It's been a long time coming. Way too late for Susan Alberti, but I'm so lucky that I get to ride one of the first footy waves.

◆ ◆ ◆

As I look to the future, being myself and helping my family are the things that drive me the most. I am so happy that I have been able to make Mum proud. My mum has looked after a lot of the people in our family over the years. But I am proud that I can financially, emotionally and physically support her now. Again, that makes me happier than anything else in the world—even more than footy.

That's what most of the money I am making from football is going towards. I have been able to give her enough money for a house deposit in February, so now she can buy a house and set herself up so that she can enjoy the rest of her life in a bit of comfort. Mum has done it so hard over the years, but I am going to try to give her the life that she deserves.

When I go and hang out with Vinny and her friends, I learn so much from them because they look at life in a simple way: they just love life. Whereas everybody else is trying to be something that they're not, or get to somewhere they don't really need to go, Vinny and her mates don't feel like they need to conform to other people's expectations. They're not hung up about buying a house by a certain age or being married before they're thirty. I really think there are lessons for all of us in the way people like Vinny see the world. Maybe we should recognise how much they can help us, rather than us thinking we are helping them.

When I think about footy, I can't help but marvel at how much the game means to me. There's no doubt, I fell out of love with it for a while in my twenties, but now it's as important to me as when I was a little kid who slept with a small Sherrin under her pillow. I'd happily watch all nine games of AFL footy every weekend if I could find the time. I think the way the game is played today is sensational.

It is so fast and skilful and tough. If you ever hear people saying that today's footy is soft compared with the old days, you should give them a nudge in the ribs and set them straight. Today's footy is incredibly tough. You have to remember that the players have never been bigger, stronger or fitter. This means they crash into harder bodies at greater speed than ever before. Our game is surely the most physically demanding code of football on the planet, but it's also the most entertaining. I love watching players take high marks and kick big goals.

I am constantly impressed by the great players like Geelong's Patty Dangerfield and Marcus Bontempelli from the Western Bulldogs. Dangerfield is like the God of footy to me. And he's such a wonderful person. One of the players I admire the most is Jordan Roughead, who played alongside Bontempelli in the Bulldogs' drought-breaking Grand Final win over the Sydney Swans. He's another great man.

The only negative thoughts I have about footy these days are when I think about having to retire one day. I wish I were invincible and could play footy forever. My greatest ambition is to play in the AFL Women's competition for ten years, which would take me to the age of thirty-eight. Who knows? Maybe my body is strong enough and I will be able to play for that long. All I know is that it will be a very, very sad day when I finally have to hang up my boots.

I am so excited by all the developments in women's footy, whether they are the AFL Women's competition or the many, many new teams starting up at grassroots level. If I can give the people running the game two messages, they are these: don't ever try to base the image of women's footy around what people look like. And make sure you look everywhere for the best players. You never know how many kids growing up in poor families all around the country might have the talent to be superstars at the highest level. These kids need to be given the opportunity for success, no matter what they look like or how much money their parents have.

Another thing that must happen is the sexuality-related stigma associated with women who play footy be gotten rid of forever.

I know there is still a whole swathe of people out there who think that every woman who plays footy is gay. That kind of stereotyping is from the Dark Ages. Seriously, why do people want to judge female athletes at all?

I know that people look at me and think that because I have short hair and tatts I must be gay. I'm sure that the people who do this have never had a strong woman in their lives. When I meet people who have that corporate straight-man look I don't start presuming they have a wife and kids. It's none of my business, anyway. People can be so quick to judge a book by its cover. That's what I hate about society and that's what I want to see change.

I am glad to say that in the last few years, since the start of the AFL exhibition matches between the Western Bulldogs and Melbourne, the focus is now more on the talent of the players. If women want to play footy—and clearly thousands of us do—then they should be able to do it without any pressure to conform to outmoded expectations. They should be allowed to be themselves. My friend Susan Alberti is right behind me on this one when she says:

> It's the women's right to play AFL football. It's not a privilege. For too long it's been considered a privilege. People saying, 'Oh well, we'll let you do it and we'll keep it quiet.' That kind of thinking is not on. It's their right to play football and they shouldn't have to go begging to anyone to get the opportunity to play football. Young women must have the choice to play whatever sport they choose. You think back to the days when the VWFL got off the ground, the women who wanted to play football were treated as second-class citizens. The best female footballers had to pay to play the

game. It just wasn't fair. Thankfully, things have now changed for the better.

The most important lesson I have learned in my life so far is to stay true to myself. I want people to know that no matter what life throws at you, just be yourself. If you want to be somebody who flies to the moon, then do that. Don't listen to anyone who tells you you're an idiot. If you're a girl and you want to play football, then play football. If you want to have dreadlocks, have dreadlocks. If you want tattoos, go and get some. Because if you get hit by a bus tomorrow, at least you're going to die knowing that you did what you wanted to do. You don't want to be like my dad on his deathbed, saying, 'I should have done this and I should have done that.' Better to know you will die having done everything that you could have done. No regrets.

I truly believe that you only live one life, and you are put on this earth to live your life in your own way. That's what I'm doing.

Moana Hope Statistics

Victorian Women's Football League

Year	Club	Games	Goals
2001	Hadfield Hawks	15	Unknown
2002	Hadfield Hawks	14	Unknown
2003	Hadfield Hawks	10	Unknown
2004	Eastern Devils	16	Unknown
2005	Darebin Falcons	18	42
2006	Darebin Falcons	18	80
2007	Darebin Falcons	18	79
2008	Darebin Falcons	17	71
2009	Darebin Falcons	15	42
2010	Darebin Falcons	1	1
2011	VU-St Albans Spurs	2	6
2012	VU-St Albans Spurs	12	45
2013	Eastern Devils	11	22
2014	St Kilda Sharks	17	87
2015	St Kilda Sharks	12	68
2016	St Kilda Sharks	20	106
Totals		**216**	**649** (since 2005)

Acknowledgements

Thanks to my family. The love, good times and acceptance from my dad, Gary, and my wonderful mum, Rosemary, and also my siblings—Ethan, Livinia, Elena, Gary (Barney), Bree, Melanie, Renee, Corey, Jamie, Shona and Jennifer—who have been so important to me. Thanks also to Kim and Ellenor—they are also sisters :)—and the rest of my family. They have made me who I am.

Thanks to my friends who have helped me through the highs and lows. To Susan Alberti, Tegan, Nicole Graves, Emily Woods, Amy C, Peta Searle and Linda Gumley.

Thanks to my footy and cricket families, past and present, including Glenroy, Merlynston Hadfield, Hadfield, Eastern Devils, Darebin Falcons, St Kilda Sharks and Collingwood Football Club, for welcoming me and Vinny with open arms, and making it so very easy to do what I love most in the world—play footy.

Thanks to my manager, James Pitcher, who has been there for me with advice, support and good cheer.

Thanks to Adam McNicol for helping me to tell my story.

Thanks to Melbourne University Publishing, to Louise Adler, Sally Heath, Louise Stirling, Perri Palmieri and Monica Svarc, for publishing my story.

And thanks also go to our supporters who have been with us from day one with their messages and attendance and support. They have shown that we are just at the very beginning of a women's footy competition that is only going to get bigger and better.